blended learning

how to integrate online
& traditional learning

kaye thorne

KOGAN
PAGE

London and Philadelphia

First published in Great Britain and the United States in 2003 by Kogan Page
Limited
Reprinted 2004, 2007

120 Pentonville Road   525 South 4th Street, #241
London N1 9JN   Philadelphia PA 19147
UK   USA
www.kogan-page.co.uk

ISBN-10   0 7494 3901 7
ISBN-13   978 0 7494 3901 9

British Library Cataloguing in Publication Data

A CIP record for this book is available from the British Library.

Library of Congress Cataloging in Publication Data

Thorne, Kaye.
    Blended learning : how to integrate online and traditional learning /
Kaye Thorne.
      p. cm.
Includes bibliographical references and index.
    ISBN 0-7494-3901-7
  1. Employees–Training of. 2. Internet in education. 3.
Computer-assisted instruction. I. Title.
    HF5549.5.T7 T4623 2003
    658.3'124–dc21

                      2002152259

Typeset by JS Typesetting Ltd, Porthcawl, Mid Glamorgan
Printed and bound in Great Britain by Bell & Bain Ltd, Glasgow

Dedication

To Louise and Mark, Sally and Dean, Marigold and Patrick for bringing fun, happiness and laughter into my summer of 2002.

Contents

Preface   *ix*
Acknowledgements   *xi*

Introduction   **1**

1. **What is blended learning?**   **5**
    Developing an employer brand   7
    So what does blended learning mean?   10
    So what are the drawbacks?   17
    Why is blended learning important?   18

2. **How to support blended learning**   **19**
    Creating the right environment for learning   19
    How do people prefer to learn?   19
    Making learning a real experience   20
    Using the whole brain   24
    So how do you get started?   28

3. **Planning ways of integrating different types of learning**   **35**
    What makes for successful blended learning?   35
    An approach to blended learning   41
    Everyone is different   43
    Helping learners to learn   47
    Creating a coaching environment   49
    Time to reflect   52

4.	**Designing blended learning**	**55**
	Creativity	56
	Tools and techniques	63
	Designing and writing online learning	66
	Contract with the learner	69
	Using other media	70
	Other key points to remember	71
5.	**Tracking blended learning**	**75**
	Inviting feedback	75
	Reflecting on learning	76
	What are the essential elements of a TNA?	80
	Using a learning management system	84
	Overcoming obstacles	84
	Areas to consider	85
6.	**Case studies**	**87**
	Rolls-Royce plc	88
	Diageo plc	92
	DaimlerChrysler UK Ltd	97
	Avis Europe plc	101
	Ashridge	104
	Basic Skills Agency	109
	Computeach International	112
	CNDL Group	113
	Nationwide Trust	115
	The US Department of Health and Human Services	117
	THINQ Limited	119
	What lessons have we learnt from the case studies?	120
7.	**Building learning networks**	**123**
	Self-knowledge	123
	Take time to talk	125
	Manage your own success	126
	Build a support network	128
	Share information	129
	Useful contacts	130

8.	**So where do we go from here?**	**131**
	What are the benefits of blended learning?	132
	What is the future for blended learning?	133
	What lessons have we learnt to date?	134
	Are you ready for blended learning?	137
	Recommended reading	*141*
	Index	*145*

Preface

When was the last time you were really excited about learning? How often do your learners feel really inspired? Have you really embraced the new learning technology?

Imagine being able to:

- undertake an online assessment that identified the way you preferred to learn;
- take that information and talk through the implications with your line manager who actually has time to spend on your development;
- select personal development actions that meet your exact learning needs;
- undertake your own development at a time, place and pace to suit you;
- only have to attend the training that you select from generic programmes to build your own personal skills base;
- work virtually and globally with your colleagues on new developments;
- track your own learning and build a personal portfolio;
- have one-to-one coaching based on your own learning needs.

Imagine the future being now. . . it is with blended learning.

Acknowledgements

Blended learning is still a comparatively new concept and I am particularly grateful to the following people for their help in clarifying the terminology and also to the individuals and companies who willingly gave their time and support in taking part in the case studies:

Mark Woodhouse, Brian Stanton, Brian Hayer, Robert B McGregor,
    Rolls-Royce plc
Claire Semple and Paul Allen, Diageo
Alix Dees, DaimlerChrysler UK Ltd
Rob Field, Avis Europe plc
Andrew Ettinger and Cath Redman, Ashridge
Steve Spanton, Computeach International
Paul Worrall, Basic Skills Agency
James Williams, CNDL Group
Jon White, Nationwide Trust Ltd
Dr Kerry M Joels, US Department of Health and Human Services
Eugene Deeny, Bena Blakeslee and Michele Cunningham,
    THINQ Ltd
Alison Church, World of Learning Conference and Exhibition

I would also like in these acknowledgements to pay tribute to my family, friends, colleagues, clients and fellow authors to whom I owe a great debt of gratitude for their ongoing care, support and inspiration:

Kelvin Harris, Matt Thorne, Louise Thorne, Andy Pellant, Alex Machray, David Mackey, Lesley Shaw, Mark Sinclair, Chris and Vivien Dunn and the whole team at TDA Transitions Ltd, Kevin McGrath, Keith Bastin, John Kenney, Alan Smith, Cheri Lofland, Ian and Rosemary Anderson, Paul Ewins, Dr Alan Stanhope, Carolin, Ross, Ben and Laura Garside, Babs Bonner, Sue and Keith Harriss, Rob and Sue Ford, Margaret and Les Ellyatt, Bill and Bernice Legg, Sid and Elizabeth Cole, Eileen and Gordon Nicholls, Charles and Jean Burrows, Diana and Nigel Gray, Joy and Peter Gunson, David, Delia and Manley Hopkinson, Elizabeth and Gordon Humphries, Pam and Alan Giblett, Angela and Steve Metcalfe, David and Helen Giblett, Sally Broadhead, Dean Farrow, Marigold Palmer Jones, Patrick Evans, Alethea Strafford, William Henwood, Steve Bedford and the Learn 2 Earn Team, Richard and Lindy Bishop, Ian Banyard, Llorett Kemplen, Sheena Matthews, Stephanie Oerton, Vivien Bolton, Peter Lightfoot, Margaret Cortis, Bill Eldridge, Chris George, Mark Gordon, Will and Anya Keith, Chris Phelps, Sheila Rundle, Doug and Lisa Twining, Joanne and David Edwards and the Kilby Family.

I also want to acknowledge the work of those who created the models and concepts that underpin many creative and innovative activities, in particular Tony Buzan for his Mind Maps® method, Peter Honey and Alan Mumford for their Learning Styles Questionnaire, David A Kolb for his Experiential Learning Model, Joseph Wallas and Jules-Henri Poincaré for their models of the Stages of Creativity, Edward de Bono for the Six Thinking Hats, Howard Gardner and his description of Multiple Intelligences, Paul Torrance for his work in highlighting the importance of creativity in education, all the authors mentioned in the Recommended reading, all the staff at the CIPD and IOD libraries for their help in compiling the bibliography, and Philip Mudd, my editor at Kogan Page, for all his ongoing inspiration and support. Finally, all the very special clients and individual learners who ultimately have been my inspiration. My grateful thanks to you all.

Introduction

This book is written for anyone who wants to create blended learning solutions. You may be any one of the following:

- a member of a training and development or HR function;

- a line manager with responsibility for on-the-job learning and development and coaching;

- an external training consultant;

- a lecturer in further or higher education;

- an e/online/blended learning designer;

- a senior executive who wishes to sponsor the introduction of blended learning within his or her organization.

Your job role may be trainer, performance coach, facilitator, developer, internal consultant, learning designer, educator or line manager. Whatever your title your interest will be in creating learning solutions that reflect and capitalize on the full breadth of learning opportunities.

WHAT IS BLENDED LEARNING?

E-learning has had an interesting impact on the learning environment. Although it represents tremendous potential in the way it could revolutionize learning and development, it has rapidly evolved into a concept of blended learning which, like its name suggests, blends online learning with more traditional methods of learning and development. This book will seek to unravel some of the mysteries that surround it and present a coherent plan for getting the best from blended learning.

Blended learning is the most logical and natural evolution of our learning agenda. It suggests an elegant solution to the challenges of tailoring learning and development to the needs of individuals. It represents an opportunity to integrate the innovative and technological advances offered by online learning with the interaction and participation offered in the best of traditional learning. It can be supported and enhanced by using the wisdom and one-to-one contact of personal coaches.

ABOUT THIS BOOK

This book is designed to provide some practical examples of how to integrate online learning with traditional learning. One of the key requirements in the implementation of blended learning is to keep an open mind and to focus on the learning experience. As many of our case study respondents mentioned, it is very easy to become excited about the potential of blended learning and to continually push the boundaries of learning further and further. Equally, because it is possible to regularly update materials, the base model can be constantly changing, which can then become confusing for learners and the people supporting them. Sometimes it is important to review and recognize what has been achieved before rushing forward again. Another key point is the need to recognize the steep learning curve that you will undertake and the need to take other people with you; senior sponsorship is particularly important.

This book is about using blended learning as an opportunity to recognize talent, harness potential, push the boundaries of personal development, and providing learning that transcends any individual or organization and puts it into a world class.

It will also help to address some key questions that you may be facing in your organization about introducing blended learning:

- What reservations do we have?

- How could we overcome these reservations?

- What can we do to help its progress?

- How will we introduce it into our organization?

- What help and support do we need to offer?

- What online learning content and learning support already exist?

- How will the content be developed?

- Will we create it or use external providers?

As well as addressing the above questions, the content is supported by case studies from organizations that have successfully implemented, or that are working towards implementing, blended solutions.

The story of blended learning will never be finished: like all learning journeys it is a continual process of discovery, but I hope you find this book useful and I wish you every success with your own explorations of blended learning.

1

What is blended learning?

One of the most important factors in creating blended learning solutions is to recognize where it fits in the broader context of organizational learning and development. Much of the underpinning concepts of learning and development have already been referenced in my previous publications, eg *Everything You Ever Needed to Know About Training* and further developed in *Personal Coaching* (full details of both books are included in the Recommended reading at the back of this book).

The potential of blended learning is almost limitless and represents a naturally evolving process from traditional forms of learning to a personalized and focused development path. What may be interesting for you is identifying where your organization is on its journey.

You may want to explore answers to the following:

- How does my organization talk about learning and development?

- How is it described?

- How is it promoted?

- What opportunities for real learning exist?

- Is the learning tailored to meet individual needs?

Blended learning, if it is to be successful, has to fit into the broader context of what else is happening in the business world, which currently has a level of uncertainty following the events of September 11 2001. However, one of the realities is that businesses are having to embrace the new technology and increasingly operate in a 24/7 global environment; their customers and suppliers demand and expect it. Sitting in the corporate boardroom can be an unnerving experience in a world where certainties are being challenged and introducing blended learning may be seen as a low priority in the corporate agenda, so developing a persuasive business case will be vital.

Importantly, blended learning should not be seen in isolation: it represents one of the most naturally evolving processes of developing your human capital. Therefore any strategy to introduce blended learning needs to be considered carefully and positioned within the broader context of not just attracting, retaining and motivating talent, but also addressing the more compelling arguments of ROI and cost savings. An important part of this consideration is based on answers to the following key questions:

- What could blended learning mean to this organization?

- How does it fit with our overall business strategy?

- How could it help us to attract, retain and motivate talent?

- What other tangible benefits could it bring us?

The businesses that will succeed in the 21st century will recognize that there is a need to do things differently. Harnessing each individual's creativity and imagination and encouraging innovation is becoming an increasingly important focus for corporate organizations. Books like *Maverick* by Ricardo Semler, once regarded as a quirky approach to organizational development, are now seen as an important stage in a passage towards doing it differently. Value-based leadership, emotional intelligence, synchronicity and intuition are no longer seen as being outside of the corporate agenda, but to be understood as an important part of individual and organizational development. Senior management are recognizing that their talent bank will be greatly depleted if they do not help people fulfil their potential.

One particular focus can be in the development of an organization, or employer brand.

DEVELOPING AN EMPLOYER BRAND

'Branding' as a generic term is often assumed to belong to the marketing function. However, organizations are increasingly waking up to the recognition that directly or indirectly most brand promises are delivered by people not products. Pick up any business magazine that talks about 'branding' and it is likely that they will be discussing the broader aspect of organizational, corporate or employer branding. There is also increasing emphasis on becoming an 'employer of choice'.

What is interesting is how this type of branding is defined. Terms like 'corporate branding', 'organizations as brands', or more recently 'employer branding', are different descriptors of basically the same process. What is clearly being recognized is that having strong consumer brands is not enough: organizations need to broaden their focus to consider other aspects such as:

■ people;

■ products/services;

■ processes/systems;

■ premises/environment.

'Branding' an organization means focusing on the key components and encouraging consistency across all functions. Like any piece of machinery, one part cannot operate without the other. Cross-functional working breaks down the traditional divisions between marketing, sales, distribution, manufacturing and HR.

The process links new service/product development and the development of employees. It links the distribution chain with the customer. It builds relationships not just agreements with external suppliers. It takes the most senior managers and involves them in the front line of the business. It puts customers in the centre and heart of the organization and builds everything else around them.

The organization doesn't just service its customers: they become its lifeblood. People do not just make promises, but they deliver, not once but over and over again, consistently developing better and better service. The organization differentiates itself in the marketplace through its people, its products, its processes and its premises.

Experience has shown that in order to develop an employer/organization brand it is important to articulate the image and vision of the future and to invite all employees to unite behind it. This 'branding' process normally has a number of components:

- *Our vision (where we want to be).* This must be a real statement that people can easily remember and identify with, not just words on a wall.

- *Our values (what we stand for/our integrity).* If these are not daily demonstrated behaviourally by everyone in the organization they are worthless.

- *Standards and practices (what we demonstrate daily).* This is the way we do things, the way our performance is measured; it applies to everyone and ensures consistency.

- *Working in partnership (the way forward).* No person or organization can function alone for long. Working with people, helping others to be successful, building pride, self-esteem and sharing success are all-important components. Equally, building close links with suppliers, encouraging the media with positive news, building links with your local community, are positive partnership actions.

- *Showing our competitors (best practice).* Be proud of your achievements, and demonstrate best practice. Be the organization that others benchmark against. This will have internal spin-offs for morale.

- *Measuring our success (real measures that everyone recognizes).* Never forget where you started; realize how much progress has been made.

- *Rewarding performance (based on success).* Not just money, but personal recognition. It is best demonstrated little and often.

- *Measuring performance (be realistic).* Not 'We promise to do our best', but 'We promise to respond within 14 days, on time, and to meet identified standards.'

- *Giving and receiving feedback (positive and constructive)*. From the bottom to the top of the organization (and vice versa) open up channels of communication.

- *Review and progress (continuously improving)*. Ask 'What have we learnt?', 'Where can we innovate?'

To prevent a distorted view of the organization the process should be seamless from the front to back and from the top to the bottom of the organization.

When asked to describe the brand of the organization, there should be a common belief based on shared vision, goals, aspirations, behaviour and practice. Everyone who is touched by your organization brand should share these common perceptions. This is not just an internal process. In the broader context of employer branding it means the way organizations position themselves externally as well as internally. This will have a particular relevance in the way organizations promote themselves in the recruitment market place, or in supplier contacts.

The most fundamental part of the process is built on behaviours, based on self-esteem, confidence and pride in the organization. People must take responsibility for meeting challenges and providing innovative and creative solutions to problems. They will then rise above the mundane and gain tremendous personal and team satisfaction from providing excellent customer service.

These concepts are not fundamentally new: what is different is gaining senior level commitment and linking all the stages together in a holistic way. By bringing all the initiatives together under an organization's 'brand concept', not only is there more coherence, there's a constant benchmark. All employees should ask the question, 'Does this action, this behaviour, this response, really reflect the brand?' and in doing so they create an organizational conscience so powerful that organizational success has to follow.

A strong brand image is as relevant to an organization as it is to a product or service. The 'people offer' behind the product has to be consistent with the brand and the commitment has to be reflected from the top of the organization to the newest recruit.

True competitive edge will be achieved by those organizations that are able to attract and retain employees and build customer loyalty through the clear transmission of the overall brand. They will be the success stories of the 21st century.

When people genuinely care for each other, when job applicants identify you as a preferred employer, you can see the pride and the self-esteem, and you know you have developed a strong corporate brand, but even more important, you know you have found the heart of your organization.

The case studies in Chapter 6 illustrate how organizations have taken blended learning and integrated it into the bigger picture of organizational development.

SO WHAT DOES BLENDED LEARNING MEAN?

One of the criticisms levelled at any sector is the use of jargon, and training and development is no different. What also happens naturally is an evolving process of development as more research is undertaken and we gain a greater understanding of a subject area. Blended learning is an example of how e/online learning has evolved from its first inception.

Current thinking would suggest that it is important to acknowledge the importance of 'learning' as much as training, so to describe the process as 'learning and development' rather than 'training and development' may be more appropriate. There have been many terms attached to learning that describe different ways of accessing learning – open learning, distance learning, programmed learning, experiential learning and more currently e/online and blended learning.

Before discussing blended learning it is perhaps helpful to identify some of the different components; first, e-learning. E-learning is provided through a variety of ways:

■ online learning programmes incorporating activities and information that are very similar to other forms of distance learning;

■ online learning portals that take people through a variety of online and offline provisions;

■ Web sites that focus on specific product and service offerings high-lighting features and benefits in the same way as a corporate brochure;

■ specific sites that allow you to download articles and tools, either free or on a free trial basis prior to purchase.

Some definitions

When one considers the e-learning component it is worth clarifying some of the language. Below is a short selection of some of the terms that you may hear. However, new descriptors are being created all the time and the only way to develop your knowledge is to talk to service providers and colleagues and always ask for clarification if you hear a term that you do not understand.

WBT (Web-based Training)

This describes training packages that are available using the Internet. Linked to this is the concept of virtual classrooms where again the Internet is used to link up different individuals in various locations with each other, and/or their tutor.

In the virtual classroom learners assemble at their own PC for a session. The material is presented to them via multimedia. In some programs there is a whiteboard facility that allows learners to contribute comments, or even draw, type text or paste images; each learner can see the end result and there are chat-rooms that allow people to talk to each other. This can be augmented by video or audio conferencing. It is also possible to share applications when learners can view or work on documents jointly, or alternatively allows learners to voice an opinion, or answer questions in a test.

Synchronous communication

Synchronous communication or learning is facilitated by bandwidth, which provides a medium similar to the way fibre optics support telephone communication. Everyone needs to be connected via an

Intranet or the Internet. Initially the sound and video quality may not be very good but as the bandwidth improves it will get better. Most communications online are asynchronous, using time-delay methods, for example email or bulletin boards.

Learning portals

These are hosted by service providers, which allow clients to access online materials held on a 'host' server. Individuals may leave a corporate Intranet and go into the Internet environment to either use one particular provider's materials, or in some cases a number of providers may be available through a portal catalogue. They may also create online learning communities. Learning portals can also be built and branded to link from a company's Intranet so that a user has seamless access from one to the other.

Learning object

One of the features of e-learning is the need to provide learning that is broken down into chunks, and is often described as 'bite-sized', or 'just-in-time'. Part of the rationale for this is that the learning often needs to be contained within a few screens as e-learners have neither the time nor the inclination to stay in front of their screens for long periods. A learning object is a way of describing these bite-sized components. They are important because they allow learners to get exactly what they need to learn, and not information that they may have already learnt in the past. This saves time in training and productivity for the learner.

Learning Management System (LMS)

An LMS provides the technology infrastructure for companies to manage human capital development by tracking employee training information and managing, tracking and launching all events and resources associated with corporate learning. A Web-based LMS provides online course and event management, content and resource manage-ment, comprehensive assessments, enhanced skills gap analysis, content authoring, email notifications, and real-time integration with human resource, financial, and ERP systems. An LMS manages all training delivery types – third party and internal – including classroom-based, e-learning, virtual classroom, technology-based training, books and video. An LMS also provides access to authoring tools, 360-degree assessments, learning content management, and/or virtual classroom functionality. See the THINQ case study in Chapter 6, or www.brandon-hall.com or www.masie.com for further definitions.

Application Service Provider (ASP)

This usually refers to a hosted service that involves 'renting' the software, for example an LMS, from an external company rather than installing it and managing it on an internal system. In addition to providing technology on a subscription basis, an ASP also provides all the IT infrastructure and support services necessary to deliver them to customers. ASPs typically host applications at a remote data centre and deliver them to customers via the Internet or a private network.

SCORM (Shareable Content Object Reference Model)

The US Department of Defense (DoD) established the Advanced Distributed Learning (ADL) initiative to develop a DoD-wide strategy for using learning and information technologies to modernize education and training. In order to leverage existing practices, promote the use of technology-based learning and provide a sound economic basis for investment, the ADL initiative has defined high-level requirements for learning content such as content reusability, accessibility, durability and interoperability.

The Sharable Content Object Reference Model (SCORM) defines a Web-based learning 'Content aggregation model' and 'Run-time environment' for learning objects. At its simplest, it is a model that references a set of interrelated technical specifications and guidelines designed to meet the DoD's high-level requirements for Web-based learning content.

The work of the ADL initiative to develop the SCORM is also a process to knit together disparate groups and interests. This reference model aims to bridge emerging technologies and commercial and public implementations.

IMS

The IMS Learning Resource Meta-Data Best Practice and Implementation Guide provides general guidance about how an application may use LOM meta-data elements. In 1997 the IMS Project established an effort to develop open, market-based standards for online learning, including specifications for learning content meta-data. For more information, see www.imsglobal.org.

Personal Digital Assistant (PDA)

This is a hand-held computer which, using WAP (Wireless Application Protocol) technology, has the potential to provide mobile access to e-learning content. This is still quite advanced for e-learning and not many companies are using it at the current time.

Knowledge management

Another word that has grown in importance is 'knowledge'; people talk about 'knowledge workers', and 'knowledge management'.

What is interesting is that this is not something that is considered as a 'soft skill'. It is about the fundamental point that 'information equals power', and in today's organizations when a relatively small number of people are developing specialist skills, should these people walk there is a very high risk of part of the business going with them.

Today's younger employees are much more mobile than previous generations. In some cases organizations are offering financial incentives to join a company, such is the need to attract new talent. Being enterprising is no longer a term just used for people who want to run their own businesses: people need to be enterprising within their own organizations.

Some of the definitions of knowledge management describe how to develop systems to manage knowledge, in the same way as you might want to keep track of intellectual capital, but the most important factor behind knowledge management is what people keep in their own head.

Increasingly people are recognizing the importance of IPR (intellectual property rights). In previous generations individuals who created new learning concepts were only too happy to just have their findings published; now those same findings could have a value attached to them.

Another source of definitions is a thought-provoking article by Brook Manville and Nathaniel Foote, 'Strategy as if knowledge mattered', a Fast Company article, April 1996. In the article they identify the following as key steps:

■ Knowledge-based strategies begin with strategy, not knowledge.

■ Knowledge-based strategies aren't strategies unless you can link them to traditional measures of performance.

■ Executing a knowledge-based strategy is not about managing knowledge; it's about nurturing people with knowledge.

■ Organizations leverage knowledge through networks of people who collaborate – not through networks of technology that interconnect.

■ People networks leverage knowledge through organizational 'pull' rather than centralized information 'push'.

Linking this to a number of case study examples of how this is put into practice, they explain that:

> These successes can be tracked to the superior use of knowledge. And they are much more compelling than the warm and fuzzy argument that companies should adopt knowledge as a philosophical goal since learning and education are 'good for the company' – or even 'good for society'. The point of a knowledge-based strategy is not to save the world; it's to make money. It's for hard heads.

When exploring the 'pull' rather than 'push' theory, they explain that the power should come from demand rather than supply and that companies run a real risk of overloading their employees with too much information. They also emphasize the importance of on-the-job 'just-in-time' learning, a term which is also used to describe some forms of e-learning. They conclude by suggesting that:

> The essence of successful knowledge-based strategies is a company's capacity to raise the aspirations of each employee. These are the people whose contributions and ongoing development becomes the life-blood of performance gains.

The implication of all this for organizations and trainers is a fundamental shift from training to learning. There is a distinct difference in ownership: the individual needs to own and take responsibility for his or her own learning, and it is important to help individuals realize their potential.

Blended learning

In my research for this book I have seen a number of descriptors but for the purpose of a working definition here, I have taken it to mean the following:

> Blended learning is the most logical and natural evolution of our learning agenda. It suggests an elegant solution to the challenges of tailoring learning and development to the needs of individuals. It represents an opportunity to integrate the innovative and technological advances offered by online learning with the interaction and participation offered in the best of traditional learning. It can be supported and enhanced by using the wisdom and one-to-one contact of personal coaches.

Blended learning is a mix of:

- multimedia technology;
- CD ROM video streaming;
- virtual classrooms;
- voicemail, email and conference calls;
- online text animation and video-streaming.

All these are combined with traditional forms of classroom training and one-to-one coaching.

There have been some concerns about the use of the word 'blended'. Too literal use of the word could imply chopping people, or creating a mush. However, there are also positive connotations to blending – coffee, perfume, whisky – that can mean the mixing together of wonderful ingredients to create something special for others to consume. Connoisseur blenders in this role need to know their customer, their preferences and how to create a mix that delights and invites them to return again and again; the more positive connotations of 'blended learning' would also mean this. Blended learning should be the ultimate perfect solution to tailoring learning to fit not only the learning need, but also the style of the learner.

SO WHAT ARE THE DRAWBACKS?

In theory there shouldn't be any. However, in reality the drawbacks can be perceived as much as real. If you want to test the theory for yourself, ask your colleagues and associates, 'What do you think of blended learning?' The following are some of the responses I've received when I've asked the question:

- 'Don't know, I've never heard the phrase.'
- 'I've heard of it, but I have no idea what it means.'
- 'Isn't it e-learning with other bits added on?'
- 'Isn't it old wine in new bottles?'
- 'Isn't it expensive?'

What is rarely heard is a clear definition, or enthusiasm about its potential. Blended learning needs enthusiasm, energy and commitment to move from the theory to the reality of developing real learning solutions based on meeting individual needs.

Other drawbacks are a lack of information and not knowing where to find it. Companies focusing on the new technology are springing up, but how do you find out who is offering what and, perhaps more important, who will offer the right services for your organization? Using e-solutions is still a relatively new approach for many organizations and like any new initiative it takes time to introduce it. With blended learning there is an additional impact of having the right infrastructure to support it. It is therefore not just a matter of identifying the right organization to deliver a programme of development. It will need a coherent and integrated plan, drawing together a number of different components. Examples of how this is done are examined in the case studies in Chapter 6.

WHY IS BLENDED LEARNING IMPORTANT?

The real importance and significance in blended learning lies in its potential. If we forget the title and focus on the process, blended learning represents a real opportunity to create learning experiences that can provide the right learning at the right time and in the right place for each and every individual, not just at work, but in schools, universities and even at home. It can be truly universal, crossing global boundaries and bringing groups of learners together through different cultures and time zones. In this context blended learning could become one of the most significant developments of the 21st century.

2

How to support blended learning

CREATING THE RIGHT ENVIRONMENT FOR LEARNING

Most good learning experiences usually take place in a special environment. By recreating the sensation of that special event learners can apply the lessons learnt then to different situations. This very much links to the concept of 'flow' (as defined by Mihalyi Csikzentmihalyi; see Recommended reading and Chapter 4 for more details); by remembering the sensation of special learning events it may be possible to enhance other learning situations. Before looking in detail at the potential of blended learning it is important to put it into the context of how people learn.

HOW DO PEOPLE PREFER TO LEARN?

Many people prefer to learn through doing or, as Kolb might describe it, 'active experimentation' (see below). Some learners prefer conversations with others, either as a sounding board, or with someone who is like-minded who could help them explore their ideas further, adding to their picture, or reshaping certain aspects of it. This also reflects the way that many people prefer to learn: discovering with others rather than being told the facts by a specialist. What is important is the need for feedback: even though individuals may want to learn through discovery they also want to know how well they are doing and to have access to coaching when they need it.

Learning is one of the most individual and personal activities that we ever undertake and yet most of us do it lumped together in learning environments that give us very little opportunity for individual coaching and support. For creative and innovative people, whatever their age, this is even harder. They crave feedback, they need time to reflect, they want very specific coaching to help them develop what they know they need to know. Unlike many others they often have a purpose to their learning and they get incredibly frustrated with what they may perceive as trivia, or irrelevant information.

We know through the work of Paul Torrance, David Kolb, Honey and Mumford, Daniel Goleman, and Howard Gardner (see below) that people respond positively to different learning stimuli, and yet many corporate environments strip out the senses. There is still so much work to do to help organizations, whether they are schools, further or higher education, or places of employment, become somewhere individuals enthusiastically want to attend.

Blended learning represents a very real step towards doing it differently and providing schools, colleges and corporate organizations with a real opportunity to make progress either in ways of working, the environment, or in giving individuals freedom to be themselves.

MAKING LEARNING A REAL EXPERIENCE

The hidden message from my school, I eventually realized, was not only crippling it was wrong. The world is not an unsolved puzzle, waiting for the occasional genius to unlock its secrets. The world, or most of it, is an empty space waiting to be filled. That realization changed my life. I did not have to wait and watch for the puzzles to be solved, I could jump into the space myself. I was free to try out my ideas, invent my own scenarios, create my own futures. (*Beyond Certainty*, Charles Handy, 1995)

Any discussion about the role and application of blended learning has to take place within the wider context of how people learn and everything that we know about the different ways this can be enhanced. You've only got to watch a group of schoolchildren on the way to school to recognize that education is so often not seen as fun. Talk to a group of teenagers trying to decide what qualifications to take, let alone what career they might want, to realize that, for most, school is a place they go to because they must, rather than because they *want*.

Many adults equate learning with experiences that they would rather forget, so awakening the learning giant within is a real challenge, but also a fantastic opportunity. There is a lot of focus on the phrase 'lifelong learning', but to achieve it takes far more than the setting up of government initiatives. It means enabling people to understand, explore and then take ownership of the learning that really matters for them. The very nature of this approach has to mean that the 'one size fits all' approach really doesn't work'. Just like the misshapen T-shirt with the label 'one size', it cannot compare to the unique tailoring and fit of a made-to-measure garment. Learning that means something important, personal and special to the individual will have far more impact than a generic learning product. So how can we apply this principle to blended learning?

First we need to set blended learning in the broader context of learning, and one of the most enduring models about learning is Kolb's learning cycle. He identified the key steps in how people learn and defined them as follows:

1. *Having an experience* – whether it is managing a project, giving a presentation, or completing a development activity. Searching out new and challenging experiences, problems and opportunities. Finding like-minded people to learn with. Making mistakes and having fun.

2. *Reviewing the experience and reflecting* on what went well and what could have been improved, as well as seeking feedback from others. Standing back from events to watch, listen and think. Listening to a wide cross-section of people with varying views. Investigating by probing, assembling and analysing information. Reviewing what has happened and what you have learnt.

3. *Theorizing about what happened and why, then exploring options and alternatives.* Questioning and probing logic and assumptions. Exploring ideas, concepts, theories, systems and models. Exploring interrelationships between ideas, events and situations. Formulating your own theories or models.

4. *Planning what to do differently next time.* Finding out how the experts do it. Looking for practical applications of ideas. Finding opportunities to implement or teach what you learn. Trying out and practising techniques with coaching and feedback.

It is important to recognize that not all learning will take place in a neat and ordered way. We learn best when we combine all four approaches to learning:

- theory input;
- practical experience;
- application of theory;
- idea generation.

Kolb's learning cycle is also linked to the work of Honey and Mumford and their Learning Styles Questionnaire:

- We all prefer to learn in slightly different ways.
- Activists learn best by doing.
- Reflectors learn best by observing.
- Theorists learn best by thinking things through in a logical and systematic manner.
- Pragmatists like to learn through putting their ideas into practice and testing them out.

To find out more detail about your or your learners' preferred learning style you may wish to undertake the Honey and Mumford Learning Styles Questionnaire. The definitions below give you some examples of the different types of learning style; try to identify which appeals to you.

Activists

- Enjoy new experiences and opportunities from which they can learn.

- Often do things first and think about it later.

- Enjoy being involved, are happy to be in the limelight and prefer to be active rather than sitting and listening.

- Often look for new challenges.

- Like to learn with people who are like-minded.

- Are willing to make mistakes.

- Like to have fun when they are learning.

Reflectors

- Prefer to stand back from events, to watch and absorb information before starting.

- Like to hear other people's viewpoints.

- Like to review what has happened and what they have learnt.

- Prefer to reach decisions in their own time.

- Do not like to feel under pressure.

Theorists

- Like to explore methodically to think problems through in a step-by-step logical way and ask questions.

- Can be detached and analytical.

- Like to be intellectually stretched and may feel uncomfortable with lateral thinking, preferring models and systems.

- Prefer to come up with their own theories or models.

Pragmatists

- Like practical solutions and want to get on and try things.

- Dislike too much theory.

- Sometimes like to find out how the experts do it.

- Like to experiment and search out new ideas that they want to try out.

- Tend to act quickly and confidently.

- Are very down to earth and respond to problems as a challenge.

You may find that you have a preference for one or two learning styles, or you may find that like a small percentage of people you have a balanced learning style. Kolb's ideas about learning and Honey and Mumford's learning styles link well together. They also link with the following model of how people learn something new:

- *Unconscious incompetence* – I don't know what I don't know and I don't know that I don't know it. Ignorance is bliss!

- *Conscious incompetence* – I know there are things that I should know, but I am not able to do them yet.

- *Conscious competence* – I know what I should know, and how to use my knowledge to put it effectively into practice.

- *Unconscious competence* – I now do things without consciously thinking about how I do them.

USING THE WHOLE BRAIN

As well as understanding your learning style you will also have a preferred way of operating, through your left or right brain. The research of Sperry and Onstein showed that we have two hemispheres in our brain, which have different characteristics or functions:

Left brain	Right brain
Logic	Rhythm
Lists	Colour
Linear	Imagination
Words	Day-dreaming
Numbers	Intuition
Sequence	Spatial awareness
Analysis	Music

If you have always primarily used one side of your brain you may find it harder to use the other. You may believe that you are no good at a particular subject; for example you may say 'I am no good at maths', or 'I've never been able to draw'. However, researchers like Tony Buzan, who developed the Mind Maps® technique, are showing that we need not be totally left-brained or right-brained, but that by using both sides of our brain in our activities we become more 'whole-brained'.

Once you understand your preferences and how you learn, you can use this knowledge to accelerate your learning, and to make your learning experiences more meaningful. If you are really interested in finding out more about how people learn you may be interested in the work of Howard Gardner.

Seven intelligences

Howard Gardner, a prominent psychologist, argues that everybody possesses at least seven intelligences:

1. *Linguistic intelligence.* The intelligence of words: these people like to read and write, play word games, they are good at spelling, verbal and written communication. They like learning from books, tapes, lectures and presentations.

2. *Logical-mathematical intelligence.* The intelligence of logic and numbers: they like experimenting with things in an orderly and controlled manner. Organize tasks into sequence. Like solving problems. They learn by creating and solving problems, playing mathematical games.

3. *Musical intelligence.* The intelligence of rhythm, music and lyrics: they may play musical instruments, often sing or hum to themselves, like relaxing to music. They learn by using music, may use rhymes to help them remember.

4. *Spatial intelligence.* The intelligence of mental pictures and images: think and remember in pictures, like drawing, painting, sculpting. Use symbols, doodles, diagrams and mind maps to learn.

5. *Bodily-kinaesthetic intelligence.* The intelligence of expression through physical activities: good with their hands. Like physical activity, sports, games, drama, dancing. Learn through doing, taking action, writing notes. Need frequent breaks when learning.

6. *Interpersonal intelligence.* The intelligence of communicating with others: these are people who are good with others. They know how to organize, relate and tune into others, put people at ease. They learn from others, like learning in teams, comparing notes, socializing, and teaching.

7. *Intrapersonal intelligence.* The intelligence of self-discovery: they prefer to work alone, like peace and quiet. Often daydream, are intuitive, keep a diary, plan their time carefully, are independent. They learn by setting personal goals, taking control of their learning, reflecting on their experiences.

Gardner also added another intelligence, naturalistic, which is generally taken to mean the intelligence that allows individuals to relate to the natural world and to classify and demonstrate a natural expertise in developing patterns, which can help the individual to develop order from chaos.

Gardner's work is also linked to the work of Daniel Goleman on 'emotional intelligence'.

Emotional intelligence

Increasingly both individuals and organizations are recognizing the richness to be found in examining areas that are more personal, such as the 'emotional competence' framework identified by Daniel Goleman in his book, *Working with Emotional Intelligence.*

Although it may seem that 'emotional intelligence' is a recent entrant into our vocabulary, it has in fact been acknowledged for a much longer period. Goleman suggests that a number of people have defined emotional intelligence, including Howard Gardner who in 1983 proposed a model of 'multiple intelligence'. Peter Salovey and John Mayer in the 1990s defined emotional intelligence 'in terms of being able to monitor and regulate one's own and other's feelings and to use feelings to guide thought and action'.

His own definition includes five basic emotional and social competencies:

1. self-awareness;

2. self-regulation;

3. motivation;

4. empathy;

5. social skills.

Goleman's work moves emotional intelligence into the arena of emotional competence by further defining 25 emotional competencies and explaining that individuals will have a profile of strengths and limits, but that:

> the ingredients for outstanding performance require only that we have strengths in a given number of these competencies, typically at least six or so, and that the strengths be spread across all five areas of emotional intelligence. In other words there are many paths to excellence.

What Goleman and others have done is to introduce the concept of another type of intelligence and suggest that our skills with people are as important to the organizations that might recruit us as our IQ, our qualifications and our expertise.

Many organizations are also recognizing the impact of this in their retention and development of key workers. These personal competencies together with other traits and characteristics present vital clues to creating meaningful learning experiences. The potential power behind blended learning is that it can connect and engage with all learning preferences and create a holistic model of personal development.

If your learners enjoy the learning experience they are more likely to learn and remember. If they are *told* they need to learn something their willingness to learn will depend on the respect that they have for the person telling them and their desire to learn. If their desire to learn is driven by a personal curiosity and they learn in a way that reflects their preferred learning style, it is likely that their own enthusiasm and interest will make the learning more meaningful and memorable. In order to create meaningful learning experiences, teachers, lecturers, trainers, workplace coaches and individual learners could do so much more to develop effective learning patterns. Ironically, much pre-school and early years learning does focus on more stimulating ways of learning, but unfortunately many of the opportunities to really experience learning seem to disappear as individuals progress through school and work.

Blended learning represents a very real opportunity to incorporate all that we know about learning as illustrated above into tailored and individual solutions that really do make valuable use of all that we know about how we learn.

SO HOW DO YOU GET STARTED?

Creating a blended solution in itself is not difficult with the right level of skills and knowledge. What may be more challenging is convincing your organization, your colleagues and your employees to adopt it and support it. To achieve that may involve you in challenging some assumptions and overcoming some prejudices or obstacles. As illustrated in the case studies, helping people recognize the full potential of a blended solution will take time and patience. It is also important to help people recognize the scale and scope of what you are developing. To plan and fully implement blended learning solutions is not something that can be approached lightly. To undertake it properly involves significant investment and commitment. It also raises the issue of how much information to share, with whom and at what stage.

When e-learning was first introduced some in-company providers and external suppliers tried to share with their customers far more information about the build than perhaps they wanted or were interested in. Our general levels of interest in the internal mechanics of the microwave oven, washing machine, or television are limited: they are pieces of domestic equipment that we take for granted until for whatever reason they don't work and then we become more interested in the different components inside them. Where blended solutions work well is where the mechanics of how the learning is constructed are less visible and instead the focus is more on the content. That is not to say it is not important to pilot and test out the prototypes of sample materials, but being involved in all the stages of the build is far less relevant.

So who needs to be involved and when?

This very much depends on the business and its internal structure. As a first step it is really important to understand and think through the implications of embarking on a process of blended learning before figuring out the who and the when. What are the immediate needs? What are the 'must haves'? Who will benefit in the organization and how will the organization as a whole benefit?

The following represents some key steps. Within this context the focus is on introducing blended learning as an overall process. Stages 7–8 may well have to be repeated for different learning interventions.

1. Strategic level discussion paper

One of the major considerations in creating blended learning solutions is the ability to enable different parts of the business to talk to each other. For example it is likely that the IT infrastructure required to support the online learning element will be developed in collaboration with the IT department. The learning components are likely to be the responsibility of the training/learning and development department. In its initial stages of development it will be really helpful for these departments to be in communication so that they are able to work together to create a discussion paper to outline the potential to the executive.

It is also important that any paper that is prepared follows the principles of any business proposal and clearly lays out the options, the business/individual benefits, the likely costs and the proposed time-scales. There should also be an executive summary.

It may be possible at this stage to gain outside support in the form of benchmarking best practice. Initial discussions with suppliers can also help in positioning the internal business benefits in the context of either your business sector, or the wider global community. In any communication it is always important to be mindful of your audience, but in this context it is even more important to make sure that the language used is accessible and not full of jargon.

It is also important that whoever presents the paper should be passionate and enthusiastic, but also knowledgeable about the content and able to make a persuasive business case. It is also important to look at the costing of the proposal within the context of other business priorities; working with suppliers on the proposed phasing of the costs can be helpful. One vital component that is often missing from the business case is the potential ROI or cost savings.

2. Sponsorship from the IT and training and development directors and commitment and buy-in from the executive

As highlighted above, if the potential has been carefully outlined with all the business advantages, it will be easier for the executive to commit to the development of blended solutions. An important aspect of this will be that, with a blended learning solution, there is the opportunity to incorporate existing learning materials and processes, but it will be inappropriate to use the executive as a committee for designing the implementation. It will be important for the directors responsible for the key areas of development to be fully briefed prior to the meeting and then they can be supportive and champion the paper when it is presented to the executive. Someone has to drive the integration, and for it to work effectively it needs support at the highest level.

Do not underestimate the need to build the case for the executive who will be making the purchase decision on new software and/or hardware. E-learning is neither cheap nor easy, so the business case needs to be made on the ROI as a result of initiating a blended programme, or the cost savings from switching to one form of training medium from another.

3. Internal champion/coordinator appointed

As well as higher level support, blended learning needs an internal champion or coordinator who will be responsible for the day-to-day integration of online learning and traditional learning. This person, or team, needs to be not only familiar with the learning processes, but also able to paint a persuasive picture of the possibilities and to be able to coordinate the different ways of learning into tailored learning solutions.

One of the very real questions you need to consider is whether you have the right expertise internally to undertake this role. This person will undergo a great learning experience, but it is important that your organization is not left exposed through lack of knowledge. If it is an internal appointment, this person needs support to enable him or her to research the market place, and it may be some time before you see a return on your initial investment, particularly in terms of the time that he or she needs to spend in potential non-contact or chargeable time.

If you do recruit externally, look very carefully at potential candidates and build a very clear role specification to ensure that you find the person who is best able to support you in developing the future.

4. Discussion paper formulated into an action plan with clear accountabilities

Like any learning development initiative it helps to be able to articulate the key stages and to outline them in an action plan and, importantly, to allocate key accountabilities. In this context it will range across a number of areas from internal marketing to individual personal development. If this action plan is linked to the planned expenditure and the potential outcomes it will be even more helpful to manage the expenditure.

Again this action plan needs to link to the overall strategic plan. It needs to be written clearly, highlighting the key points, any jargon needs to be clarified and it needs to be set in a business context.

Include a schedule in the action plan and do not underestimate the time it takes to implement certain solutions. Find out from the technology provider the realistic time needed to implement a particular solution. It is also important to consider the scale of project. Large implementations often follow a phased approach, in order to address the immediate training needs and then bring on more technology and learners as the implementation progresses.

5. Internal cross-functional team selected to work on creating blended solutions

One of the very real issues in the early days of the development of online learning was a lack of understanding of the potential of the technology available and as highlighted elsewhere in this book, some of the early attempts were nothing more than taking the text from a book or training programme and putting it on a screen. To achieve meaningful blended solutions it is really important to consider carefully the range of media available and to create the best possible solutions. This is not something that can be achieved overnight: if something is put together in a rush and then doesn't work the impact on the likely internal support can be enormous. It is far better to work at creating successes, which can be piloted, reviewed and then learnt from.

It will also be important to help this team develop the broadest understanding of the range of learning opportunities that could be created using blended solutions. People in this group need open minds and must not take fixed positions based on their own preferences.

6. Undertake an audit of the current learning provision, analyse who is doing what to whom and create a relationship database

One of the real issues within large organizations is gaining a full picture of what is happening within learning and development within the business. This is further complicated if, as with many large organizations, some of the responsibility for purchasing learning and development has been passed down into the business. The larger the organization the wider the span of control. Introducing blended learning can provide an opportunity to undertake an audit of all the learning solutions that are available within the organization.

This is a very valuable activity: not only can it yield useful information about what is currently being undertaken within the organization, it can also form the basis of the analysis of what would lend itself to online learning and what needs to stay with more conventional forms of learning. There is a real advantage in undertaking this before working with any external providers as it will ensure that you have a clear base from which to position any new developments.

7. Undertake research to identify key providers of online learning

Online learning is still a comparatively new offering, and identifying excellence can be difficult. Like any form of learning and development it will be important to undertake research to identify providers who can meet your criteria. Follow the same processes as you would in any other context. Talk to colleagues both in and outside the business, read journals and use the Internet to identify names of key providers. If you have very little knowledge of online or blended learning, talk to more than one provider, talk to fellow professionals who may have more experience, contact your professional bodies, look in the relevant trade journals. Attend industry trade shows to get hands-on knowledge of the different providers you are investigating: this is also a good way to interact with peers and experts in the industry. You may also want to consider sharing your own experiences in implementing blended learning (see Chapter 7).

It is essential that you talk to companies that have direct relevant experience in implementing blended solutions. Not all e-learning providers have knowledge of blended learning. Also, it is vital that the provider chosen can demonstrate they are able to work in partnership with a number of other providers and are happy to share methodology. Although it may initially seem confusing, it is important that you really understand what the providers are offering. Take time to identify exactly what the different services mean – some of the definitions are highlighted in Chapter 1, but new terms and services are being developed all the time and it is really essential that you keep up to date if you are going to commission or use e-learning. Do not be concerned about asking what you feel may be 'dumb' questions: implementing blended learning solutions still represents a steep learning curve for many people.

8. Try to refine this list to invite three to five external providers to tender to provide a blended solution

It is not necessarily the case that will you go outside of your organization to build blended solutions. However, many organizations do not have the essential expertise internally to handle the total implementation. Part of the selection process will involve identifying what support is really needed; this will vary enormously from one organization to another and may consist of you identifying the exact level of support required. This may include commissioning a Learning Management System (LMS) or buying an off-the-shelf online learning solution, or commissioning your own tailored content.

Part of the preparation of the tender document will be to identify exactly what you hope to achieve, and this is when the knowledge and experience of the internal coordinator will be important. If you do not have this knowledge and expertise in house, you may wish to consider using a consultant to help you through these early stages and to provide benchmarking information for you. There is now more knowledge available about blended learning, which could help you put together the tender document and list of key questions for the providers. The culture of the provider organization you are selecting is also important. Software implementations can be lengthy so you need a provider who will partner you every step of the way.

Once you have selected your provider there then follows the next phase of development, which is to start the implementation of a process of generating blended learning solutions. This is detailed in Chapter 3.

3

Planning ways of integrating different types of learning

WHAT MAKES FOR SUCCESSFUL BLENDED LEARNING?

In reality the underpinning principles of blended learning are no different from any other form of learning. The key criteria are based on the following:

1. Identifying the core learning need.

2. Establishing the level of demand/timescale.

3. Recognizing the different learning styles.

4. Looking creatively at the potential of using different forms of learning, ie matching the learning need to different delivery methods and identifying the best fit.

5. Working with the current providers, internal and external, to identify the learning objectives and to ensure that the provision meets the current need.

6. Undertaking an education process and developing a user-friendly demonstration to illustrate the potential of blended learning.

7. Being prepared to offer follow-up coaching support.

8. Setting up a monitoring process to evaluate the effectiveness of the delivery.

1. *Identifying the core learning need*

Identifying the learning opportunity in blended learning is the same as identifying any learning opportunity. However, what is important is recognizing the need to provide the right solution for your learner.

One of the real advantages of blended learning is the opportunity to be more focused and specific about the learning need. Increasingly organizations are recognizing the importance of tailoring learning to the individual rather than applying a 'one size fits all' approach. We all have preferred ways of learning and despite all the research and recommendations to take account of how people learn, many organizations from school to work still continue to provide blanket solutions.

As training solutions evolve into learning solutions the hope is that organizations will begin to recognize the importance of making the learning more appropriate for each individual. Blended learning provides a great opportunity to really tailor the learning to the learner. Of course there will be common themes, common needs, but there is also the opportunity to look creatively at how the learning experience is designed and to use a variety of media to suit differing needs. At this stage it will also be important to consider how your organization will adapt to the online learning component of blended learning. Not all organizations have the infrastructure to support this type of learning. Find out what works best in your company's culture.

At this stage it is also important to identify how you are going to create the different parts of the solutions. There will be a number of ways in which the learning objectives can be met, and it will be essential that whoever is responsible for commissioning the solution has the necessary ability to look creatively at all the options. This particularly links to how the learning might be tailored. For example, if you have a generic need it may be possible that an off-the-shelf provision could be purchased. This could be supported by personal coaching by a line manager who could prepare the learner prior to him or her undertaking the learning experience and following it up afterwards. In this way the overall learning experience will feel more personalized.

2. *Establishing the level of demand/timescale*

In any decision about developing learning solutions there will always be a need to assess the reality of the demand. However, blended learning represents a real opportunity to respond more effectively to individual demand and as such has an application that is as relevant to an individual within a very small business as it is to a team of learners in a large global company. The very nature of the blend builds in flexibility. As with the development of any learning solution it will be important to gain a real understanding of the shape and scale of the demand, not just currently but also in the future. This highlights the importance of making sure that whoever is identifying the learning needs really understands blended learning so that they are able to ask the deeper-level questions to understand not just the immediate learning needs, but the future needs too. It will also help if they can explore with the sponsor the potential of creatively offering different approaches to learning including the full range of blended options. This is explored in more detail later in this chapter and in Chapter 4.

3. *Recognizing the different learning styles*

We know through the work of Kolb and Honey and Mumford that we all have preferred learning styles. As well as considering the different learning styles there are other factors to take into consideration in the way that people prefer to learn, as discussed in Chapter 2. A blended learning solution needs to take account of these factors. In fact a positive by-product of using blended learning is that it provides a range of learning solutions. It also represents a great opportunity to review and revitalize the full learning and development offered. Use blended learning to ask yourself or your team the question, 'How could we really do things differently?'

4. *Looking creatively at the potential of using different forms of learning*

One of the biggest criticisms about e-learning was that many of the early examples were either text driven by technology, or technology driving text. In the former the criticism was that people had simply taken words and put them on the screen with little thought about the real creative opportunities offered by the technology. Another criticism was about the Web designers who got carried away with the wizardry behind text manipulation and particularly animation only to find that learners were unimpressed or frustrated by the time it took to download learning objects.

Like most learning initiatives, integrating blended learning represents an opportunity to take what exists and evolve it into a different dimension using new technologies. One of the first steps is identifying what exists. This can be a comparatively simple or a more complex exercise. In large or global organizations it can be difficult to keep up to date with local developments. Learning and development professionals are a creative breed and a programme that may have been developed centrally may often evolve into something quite different as it is rolled out into local regions and districts, or even into different functions.

'Tailoring' to meet the needs of customers can mean that the approach or content may be different to the original. Equally the wisdom gained through implementation may mean that what is offered is different from the original interpretation. All of this normally represents the healthy stages of implementation and development.

This is where blended learning can really come into its own, by presenting the learner with a wide range of options. An important part of this process will be based on all the key stages above; in particular the level of demand will be an important factor in designing the solution.

5. *Working with the current providers to identify the learning objectives*

In many large organizations this represents the toughest challenge particularly if the different provisions are located in different parts of the organization either geographically or psychologically. IT implementation and creating an e-environment may not necessarily sit next to learning and development. If you are a strong advocate of classroom training, a facilitator or a one-to-one coach you may not necessarily look for an online learning solution. The power of blended learning is that it can enable more elegant and bespoke solutions by combining one or more methods. The secret is to really analyse what the key learning needs are and the most appropriate way of meeting them. In the early stages it may need some really basic examples of how it could work. (See later in this chapter and the case studies in Chapter 6.)

One of the challenges may be helping others adapt to the new forms of learning. If you feel that you excel in stand-up training you may be less enthusiastic about adopting different ways of developing others. If you are fascinated by the use of design and technology in developing learning solutions you may be less aware of the different ways that learners learn. In today's learning environment there have been a number of changes including using the line manager as coach, shorter training sessions and the use of online learning and multimedia packages. Going forward it will be important to help everyone involved with learning and development to make their maximum contribution.

6. Undertaking an education process and developing a user-friendly demonstration

As well as highlighting the need to outline the potential of blended learning, there is also the need to undertake an education process with the rest of the business. This will need to be far-reaching as it will include fellow learning and development professionals, line managers and the learners themselves. Some of the potential issues are likely to be linked to the need to do things differently and supporting people with handling change, so it will be important to help people recognize the potential as well as helping them to identify the solution that works for them. There are a number of ways that this can be achieved: online demonstrations, PowerPoint presentations, small lunchtime meetings or workshops. Ways of achieving this are highlighted in the case studies in Chapter 6.

7. *Being prepared to offer follow-up coaching support*

Before e-learning became so topical some organizations had created learning resource centres, in some cases investing large sums of money in purchasing or developing multimedia solutions. These centres provided learners with the opportunity to use technology to support their learning and development. One of the factors that determined the success or otherwise of these centres was the level of support available. This has remained an issue throughout the development of e-learning and blended learning.

As discussed in Chapter 2, there needs to be support available to help the learner work through the different aspects of blended learning. This support does not have to be through the same person: it could be a line manager who starts the process and continues to monitor progress throughout the individual's development. The individual may also have a mentor, and can be encouraged to talk through his or her life goals with someone close. There may be an online support coach, peer support teams or different tutors linked to both the online and classroom development. The important point is that when learners feel the need for support they have access to the most appropriate person available for them.

8. *Setting up a monitoring process to evaluate the effectiveness of the delivery*

One of the criticisms levelled at many learning and development initiatives is that they are not effectively monitored and evaluated. This can have significant impact when the organization is trying to measure the ROI. With something as far reaching as introducing blended learning it is important to track the development, the lessons learnt and what improvements can be made. Having an internal learning management system can really help in this process; see an example in the case studies in Chapter 6. Evaluation is discussed in more detail in Chapter 5.

AN APPROACH TO BLENDED LEARNING

1. Identifying the core learning need

Line managers need to be trained as coaches and to identify the key components of the learning. In this case, there is quite a wide range: some of it is related to underpinning skills development, for example communication skills such as questioning, listening and giving feedback. They could do some background reading, identifying and using some tools and techniques such as SMART and GROW, and practise using the coaching process and receiving feedback.

2. Establishing the level of demand/timescale

The company is committed to creating a coaching culture, therefore they want to train all managers with a development programme that will be delivered company-wide over a two-year period.

3. Recognizing the different learning styles

The managers will all have different learning styles and the programme needs to cater for this.

4. Looking creatively at the potential of using different forms of learning

At present a 'Train the coach' programme is being rolled out but the programme lasts three days and take-up is limited, as it is difficult to release managers for that length of time. Therefore a blended learning approach could be an ideal solution. Construct a storyboard or flowchart detailing the key steps and the required knowledge at each step. Some of the theory could be delivered online or using a CD-ROM, which could be tested with an online assessment. Video-streams of coaching scenarios could be developed with observation sheets as offline support. Following the pre-work, the managers could then attend a shortened training programme to practise the skills, and this could be followed up by coaching support in the workplace. Refresher material could also be available online if at any time they wanted to go back into the knowledge components. As well as technical helpline support there could be email support for queries that they might have. They could also form a support network online.

5. *Working with the current providers to identify the learning objectives*

Present the solution to the learner and refine the offering. The solution should be reviewed with the overall owner of the solution and matched against the original request and objectives. Ideally it should be piloted with a representative sample of people. Sometimes if there is time pressure this stage can be omitted in the rush to implement. However, even if this is the case the learning can be identified as the solution is implemented and feedback mechanisms built in. By ignoring this stage the overall solution may be less effective. Organizations and departments can sometimes be in too much of a hurry to present the solution in its finished state, and time for amendments should be built into the overall schedule.

6. *Undertaking an education process and developing a user-friendly demonstration*

There will be at least two audiences: the original sponsor of the training and the line managers themselves, as well as the trainers currently delivering the programme. All will need to be convinced of the value of undertaking a different process.

7. *Being prepared to offer follow-up coaching support*

With a reduced course component it will be important to support the managers before the course to outline the objectives, and to be available to give support when they start putting their own coaching process into practice.

Make it very clear what help is available, and distinguish between technical helpline support and coaching support. Both should be readily available, particularly in the early days of implementation.

8. Setting up a monitoring process to evaluate the effectiveness of the delivery

It is important that the learners' needs are fully captured and documented at the start of the project and that any success measures are based around these. As with traditional learning, there should also be objectives defined for blended learning solutions. Also seek to gain objective feedback from those involved in the blended learning about their response to the learning and seek to incorporate their findings into the overall design. It could also be extremely valuable to test out the approach on those who have already been trained with a more traditional method, asking the question, 'If you had been trained in this way, what would you have liked, or wanted to be changed?' (see the Avis example in Chapter 6).

More examples of blended learning in practice can be found in Chapter 6.

EVERYONE IS DIFFERENT

Everyone *is* different and gaining an understanding of the differences is essential if you are to create blended learning solutions. Recognizing these differences is an important part of helping others to learn. What is fascinating is recognizing how subtle these differences are. No two people will have exactly the same combination, and in this context we should never make broad assumptions about different learners.

One way that you can help individuals gain personal insight is by encouraging them to build an understanding of themselves. One phrase that sums this up is 'being comfortable with yourself', which is used to describe the inner confidence that comes from knowing your strengths and areas of development. With this inner confidence also comes an ability to accept challenges and to want to explore personal boundaries and comfort zones. Without this understanding there is a danger that the learner may not be able to respond positively to feedback from others.

We can build a picture of ourselves through a variety of means, but the model shown in Figure 3.1, which is adapted from the original model found in *Everything You Ever Needed to Know About Training*

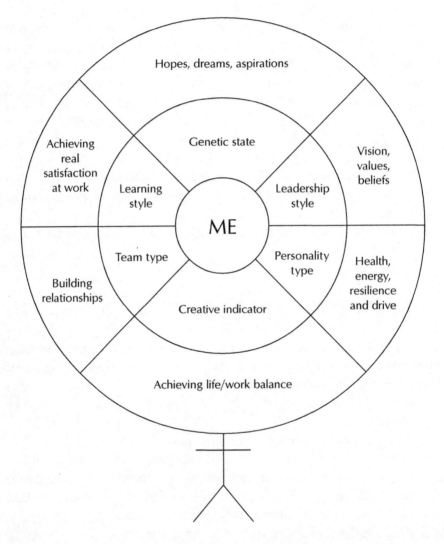

Figure 3.1   © The Inspiration Network

(Thorne and Mackey, 2001) and is one of the key models in my book, *Personal Coaching* (see the Recommended reading list), illustrates the type of analysis that we can undertake to gain a clearer picture of ourselves, and even more important, how others perceive us.

Traditionally discussion around these areas has normally only occurred at the point when someone is being made redundant and a redundancy counsellor may have encouraged an exiting employee to think about the implications of being made redundant, on their family, their lifestyle and their finances.

However, if you are going to develop an holistic approach to blended learning all these additional areas are really important in helping the individuals take charge of their lives and to see their learning in the broader context of their work and lifestyle choices.

When working with a learner we can build on this picture by probing deeper into particular areas, encouraging them to undertake reputable psychometric tests or personal profiling tools. In addition help them to make linkages between the outcomes, exploring with them the implications of this information in the way that they achieve their personal goals, or the impact of this on the way they work with others. Importantly, help the learners realize that this model of them is not static: lifetime learning will help them to develop new layers of knowledge and understanding.

What blended learning can do is help them to identify their start point and work with them to build a picture of themselves which can then form the basis of an integrated approach to learning that can become as personal and unique as their own thumbprint. If you then support this learning with targeted and focused coaching, the learning really does become a very special experience.

Analysing development needs

In working with individuals it is important that you help them to recognize that *who* they are will impact on *what* they want to do and *how* they are able to achieve their goals.

By undertaking psychometric tests or profiling you will help them gain insight into who they are, but by encouraging them to recognize

45

the impact and importance of the outer circle you will enable them to view their own development in the context of the bigger picture.

Within the context of the model it is important to recognize that this is only the top level of an underpinning skill, knowledge and competence set and once the key areas are analysed, then you can work with the learner to identify key areas of development.

The inner circle

This circle is created to illustrate some of the areas where psychometric and profiling tests can measure preferences and the underpinning personality and characteristics of an individual learner. What is important is not necessarily the specific areas highlighted but to identify a range of tools that will serve to give individuals feedback that helps them to identify who they are.

It is important to help learners to recognize that this can only be a snapshot in time. This knowledge is enhanced and developed through feedback.

The outer circle

The areas identified here are one version of how you could encourage your learners to review some of the key aspects of their personal development. Under each of these groups of questions there are a series of sub-questions followed by a means of building up the skills and competencies into a development plan.

Sometimes when individuals survey their wheel of life they feel quite daunted by the total picture and in this context this illustrates how a blended learning approach could support their personal development.

Some areas are more personal than others and they may need to work through some of them with a personal coach. It may not be appropriate to discuss an individual's finances, or the long-term care solution for an aged relative, or a deep issue in their personal relationship. What is important is that you enable your learners to recognize that it is a factor that they have to consider and that if they put time aside to address the issue it will help them in other aspects of their life.

HELPING LEARNERS TO LEARN

It is important to consider how online and blended learning can be incorporated into an organization. It should not be an either/or but rather a supplement to other types of training and learning.

For an industry devoted to developing others, sometimes great divides can develop between different functions or disciplines.

Helping you to help others

There are so many ways in which you can develop your own skill set to enable you to help others. The very nature of blended learning is based on the traditional ways that people have always learnt. There are the underpinning skills of effective communication, observing, questioning, listening and giving feedback, but there are also a range of other online techniques that provide a richness and depth of knowledge that was not possible with some traditional methods.

As you grow in knowledge you can help a learner to take the steps along their road to fulfilling their potential, and everyone involved in supporting learners should be aspiring to match the learning to the learning style. What blended learning provides us with is the opportunity to review very carefully our learning provision and to design solutions that play to the strength of each medium. It shouldn't become a 'turf war' – 'My classroom training is better than your distance learning package, my coaching is better than your online learning package.' Blended learning presents us with a real opportunity to both analyse what exists and revisit our provision; it also may challenge our assumptions about how learning can be delivered.

So what is the role of the trainer?

Supporting blended and online learning involves rethinking the role of the tutor, but it can also open up opportunities to coach and offer support. You can also develop materials, and 'e-tutor' through the virtual classroom. By rethinking some of the knowledge aspects you can make the actual physical training events very special.

It is important for trainers to identify where their provision fits within the learning cycle. Their input fits within the overall concept of knowledge transfer – inspirational trainers can by the nature of their skills and competencies inspire others through their words and behaviours. This transfer of knowledge we know can be enhanced by helping people learn through their senses. Therefore the more the trainer involves learners in their learning the more effective it will be. Although we know the power of learning through doing, there is also value in learning through presentation. A skilful and effective trainer will be closer to the role of the storyteller who can enthral and prompt deep thought and imagination – but however inspiring they are the limit of this presentation should be about 20 minutes.

A trainer designing and orchestrating a perfectly balanced event will need to provide a wide range of learning opportunities. Unfortunately too many learners are still being subjected to large classrooms of training content delivery, which only really serves the purpose of recording attendance, ie my body is in the room, but my mind and spirit are elsewhere.

The real role of the trainer is to recognize what the learner needs to learn through classroom learning and to identify the value-added benefits. As part of this analysis it will be important to look at each area of content and ask, 'What is the most effective way of delivering this learning?' and to look at the overall content and identify whether the needs of people with different learning styles are being met.

The role of the line manager

Increasingly line managers are being encouraged to play a role in learning and development, and a blended learning environment could provide very helpful support. Using a combination of learning could ensure that the line manager is able to tailor and focus the learning to meet the needs of all of his or her team. Developing the macro-enabling skills of facilitation, coaching and giving feedback could provide line managers with a set of core skills that can be used in a variety of situations. As part of this development, if they are also encouraged to practise questioning, listening and observing they will feel better equipped to identify the real development needs of their team. Finding the right solution could be a combination of using internal and external provision, online learning and their own coaching support as the learner puts it into practice.

One of the issues for line managers, in the same way as anyone else in the business, will be the identification of the relevant sources of learning and development. The accessibility of online learning can be a problem unless the company provides an infrastructure of appropriate technological support.

CREATING A COACHING ENVIRONMENT

As highlighted in Chapter 1, the corporate world is changing quite dramatically: businesses are facing challenges on an unprecedented scale and the retention of key employees is a major ongoing issue. Employees equally are looking for organizations that value their contribution.

One major way of helping all individuals fulfil their potential is to develop a coaching environment. This is not something that will not be achieved overnight, but if you can engender a sense of sharing wisdom you are more likely to create a real sense of personal development. This is very different from the process of 'managing' and could play a major role in the successful implementation of blended learning.

A coach guides rather than manages; throughout history there have been instances of guidance being given by 'elders'. What if instead of creating 'managers' we created guides? What if we gave respect to the wisdom of our experienced workers? The very best supervisors and managers are those who share their wisdom and give guidance to new employees. The very worst managers are those who play it by the rules with no flexibility or explanation.

Introducing a coaching environment may have a very far-reaching impact; individuals need to think about their very best learning experiences, to remember what inspired them, to think about how they can recreate special learning. Managers need to forget about being in control, instead helping their team members to explore by asking open questions and being provocative. Although individuals should never be taken unsupported outside their comfort zone they can be encouraged to push their boundaries beyond their normal learning experiences. Equally trainers could also perform the role of a coach and may need to recognize that in the future classroom training may become much more focused on the individual, and as a result there may be more small discussion groups or one-to-one coaching than classroom sessions.

Traditionally coaching was something that might have only been offered to senior executives or fast-track employees. However, as more and more people become aware of the benefits of one-to-one support coaches may be found operating at a number of levels within an organization. A major advantage is that if people really begin to adopt coaching behaviours the organization becomes much more of a learning environment and people start to learn from each other. However, it needs attention to survive. Too many employees are introduced to an idea, process and way of working, only to find that it is not sustained.

Personal coaching could be described as enabling, ie supporting another individual to achieve his or her personal goals. Within this context it uses a skill set that is similar to mentoring or counselling. To coach someone successfully it is likely that you will draw on the skills of questioning, listening, observing and giving feedback, and will work within a coaching model of support and challenge. The difference between personal coaching and coaching is similar to the concept of a personal sports trainer: the coaching offered very much focuses on the needs of the individual, it is driven by the individual and often looks holistically at his or her needs as opposed to being purely work-related.

Often a plan is worked out between the coach and the participant, which sets personal goals and targets and enables the participant to prepare for and take control of challenging situations. It is often very proactive and the relationship is built up over a period of time, which enables the coach to really develop a 'support and challenge' approach.

The role of the personal coach

Being a personal coach is like accompanying someone on a journey; being described as a personal guide could be more accurate. As in any journey it is important to prepare, to have an overall sense of direction and then to build in special stepping stones. In acting as a guide there is the need to recognize that at certain times the individual will want 'guidance' and at other times will be ready to enjoy a process of self-discovery. As coaches we have a responsibility to get close to our learners and to help them to know themselves. By understanding how people learn and building that knowledge in those whom we coach, we are actively demonstrating the slogan, 'Give a man a rod and teach him to fish.'

As a personal coach you will find yourself using a number of techniques, many of which are used in other applications, for example counselling, mentoring, facilitating or managing others. What is important is the way in which you use the right techniques for the right people, and also the way in which you build the coaching relationship so that the individual is not aware that you are actually using techniques, and the interaction feels natural.

A personal coach is someone with whom individual learners can develop an ongoing relationship, which enables them to explore their personal thoughts in more depth – someone who will help them to achieve insights, who will continue to be there for them over a period of time. In many ways this person is a guide, or helper, or fellow traveller.

Right time, right place, right person

This does not just apply to the development of your skills as a personal coach: it also has a relevance to your own learning. The skilled partner will delight in your learning, he or she will help you to move forward with encouragement, giving you positive feedback. The experience is different, it's memorable and it forms an important part of your development. Find the right time, the right place and the right person to guide your personal understanding and it will enable you to experience learning that is so profound that the memory will stay with you forever.

When personal coaching is done well it:

■ creates rapport;

■ sets the right environment;

- is part of an ongoing relationship;
- focuses on the individual;
- shares mutual respect and provides the opportunity to learn from each other;
- applies higher-level skills/competencies;
- allows actions to be agreed and followed up.

The role of the personal coach, tools and techniques are discussed in much more detail in *Personal Coaching* (see the Recommended reading section).

TIME TO REFLECT

As highlighted in this and the preceding chapters, introducing blended learning represents a very positive opportunity to develop personalized and stimulating learning. However, it is not something to contemplate without recognizing your own and your organization's starting point. Below are a series of questions designed to prompt reflection and hopefully highlight some key areas of development, which could make your implementation more effective:

- How often do we take time to think through projects properly?
- Do we use planning techniques?
- Do we have analytical thinking skills?
- We will need to plan this process. Have we undertaken a SWOT analysis yet?
- How creative are we? Are we hungry for information? Are we curious?
- Do we share ideas with others, do we take advantage of global time-zones to work virtually in teams?
- Do we use idea-generating techniques? Do we take time to identify what really inspires us?

■ How open are our minds? How often do we say, 'Why don't we try this?' rather than, 'We've tried it before, it won't work'?

■ What do our customers need that we don't currently give them?

■ What do we have that works really well that could be adapted? What could we do quicker? More efficiently?

■ Do we build teams of people with different styles of thinking? Do we take time to explore how we can work together? Do we play to people's strengths?

■ Do we tend to keep to the same pattern of working, or do we regularly explore new options?

■ When we are presented with a challenging situation, do we take time to explore the 'what if' and develop a plan for contingencies?

■ Do we develop a 'worst case' scenario and plan how we would deal with any issues that might arise?

■ When testing possible links, do we ask who, what, why, when, where and how, and consider all possible consequences of new product development and project management?

■ Do we always consider the bigger picture?

■ Do we consider the strategic implications, the people implications, and the customer?

■ How often do we review the decisions that we have made?

■ Do we allow time to review our assumptions before passing on our conclusions or decisions to others?

■ Are we driven by a deadline or do we build in a contingency time that allows for reflection and consultation?

You may want to reflect on these questions, or discuss the key issues with another team member or colleague. The next chapters focus on some of the issues raised here.

4

Designing blended learning

When I get together with other musicians for a jam session, the group starts with a theme, plays with it, and passes it around. Suddenly the music lifts off, flies. We all fly with it. . . It's an explosion of inspiration within art's given universe. No matter how high we fly we always return with something new, something we have never heard before. That's jamming. The management of creativity is rich in such paradoxes. It is both an art and a discipline. . . Jazz starts with a whim, a possibility, a 'gut feel'. If the whim continues to interest us we play with it. Our playing makes analogies and comparisons, entertains contradictions and variations. Development occurs. We get emotionally involved. . . All this is risky. Unavoidably so, when the alto sax player starts a solo he doesn't know where he is going, let alone how and for how long. His inner voice – to which the music, other players, the setting, even the listeners contribute – direct him. That is the nature of improvisation and companies that aren't willing to take its risks are not long for this fluid, protean, constantly challenging world. (Kao, *Jamming. The art and discipline of business creativity*)

Designing blended solutions means much more than just identifying the learning need and commissioning a provider to create a solution. The most meaningful solutions will be created by those who really explore the full potential of how people learn and work with creativity and imagination to provide rich and stimulating learning experiences. One of the key stages in achieving this is to explore the creative process.

CREATIVITY

Creativity is one of those words that prompt very different reactions from different people. For some their eyes glaze over as if you are about to enter one of those 'soft areas' where they feel very uncomfortable. For others it prompts strong debate: 'You can't teach creativity, people either have it, or they don't.' Alternatively, those who have experienced the power of being in 'flow' talk powerfully about how special the experience is.

Pure creativity often has to fight through so much rubbish and junk: accumulated facts that were given to us through our education that we have never used, junk mail, emails, memos or meetings that we have to attend. Through the window beckons a vial of inspiration essence if only we could reach out and pick it up.

It is hard to anchor down some of the key points that need to be explored and much of this is because creativity is about feeling. Creative people when inspired have an energy: they often use their senses; they often operate through multiple intelligences. It can also be a tiring experience: they may lock themselves away for hours working on an idea or a project.

People who naturally enjoy exploring their creativity do see life through a different optic. They may be driven by a force that gives them an energy that others cannot quite comprehend. They have a passion to make something work, to find a new way of doing things. They often want to 'make a real difference' not just within their own working environment, but something for the greater good for the organization, or humanity in general. In pursuit of this they can become completely absorbed, and very frustrated when others do not have the same passions. This can be particularly true when waiting for a response or feedback from others: because they invest so much personal energy and time in an embryonic idea, it can very hard for them to then have to wait while their idea goes through a bureaucratic process before they get a decision about the acceptance of their idea. This often prompts creative individuals to leave an organization and to work for themselves.

The trouble is that traditional organizations are not the most forgiving of environments. In many firms, failure carries the corporate equivalent of the death penalty. If you make a mistake, corporate Siberia beckons. This sends a signal to the corporate system that failure is punished. This not only stops people from failing – it stops them from trying. It leads to the building of systems that act against innovation rather than ones that nurture innovation. True innovators are prepared to fail in pursuit of unknown territory – terra incognita instead of terra firma... Traditionalists should remember the only way not to fail is not to try. And try we must. (Ridderstrale and Nordstrom, *Funky Business*)

One of the toughest parts of being driven by your creative thoughts is controlling it and channelling it into a normal working environment. The outpourings of ideas that are full of richness cannot necessarily be managed within the confines of a normal working day. As a result, where an individual is expected to work within the constraints of a time-frame, frustration and tiredness and ultimately lack of motivation often occur. What do you do when you find that your mind is racing at 2 am particularly if it is focusing on a non-work related subject that is close to your heart and you know that the next morning you are expected to attend an internal meeting that will sap all the remaining energy you have? All you want to do is to stay with the idea that demands your attention. This is a challenge faced by all creative people, along with the need to respect and acknowledge the needs of others. What is interesting is that if you have the inner flow of energy or ideas you need very little to stimulate it.

Mihalyi Csikzentmihalyi, a University of Chicago psychologist, described this feeling as 'flow'. He says that we experience 'flow' when we feel in control of our actions and are masters of our own fate. He discovered that when people were experiencing 'flow' there was a sensation of pleasure: they felt as if they were floating, they were totally immersed in what they were doing, they forgot their worries and lost sense of time. One of the challenges is to focus, to capture all the richness before the ideas dry up or we are interrupted.

Many people feel that their best ideas occur when they are least expecting it, or doing something else. However, once they start to flow they want to try to capture them, to record everything, as even the most insignificant points may ultimately become an important feature of the end result. If the ideas are not flowing it is important not to force the process: it is better to leave it and do something else. Often people find that by doing something completely different their mind will suddenly start generating ideas. Creative thinking also takes place at night through something called the Theta process, which is when the mind produces its own solutions that are there when you wake up. If you expose yourself to richness of experience you can stimulate your creativity by drawing down from external stimuli and other pleasurable experiences.

Identifying sources of inspiration

If you are a trainer, teacher, coach or learning designer you may spend almost all of your working life helping others to soar, but what about you? When was the last time that you thought about your own hopes, dreams and ambitions?

If you want to learn how to soar, before you take off you need to draw on your innate wisdom about yourself and to really explore your potential to help you reach your greatest heights. How well do you know yourself? How far do you push the boundaries of discovery? What do you do to inspire yourself?

Inspiration is sometimes hard to define: you cannot easily anchor it down and look at it. It is a sense, a feeling, a mood, something that lifts you above the ordinary and enables you to achieve something special. To be inspired transcends the normal day-to-day activities.

'What are the best conditions that help you to be creative/innovative?' This was one of the questions in a survey I undertook for my book *Managing the Mavericks* (see Recommended reading for details). The responses reveal a richness of stimuli, ranging across outside environments to organizational teams and an individual's own domestic space. A number of respondents give examples of when they are in 'flow'. Freedom is often mentioned, as is feeling relaxed, and when discussing preferred working environments, a need to be stimulated through their senses. Other people are important for some respondents, either as a sounding board, or just being around to talk to, socialize with, or to be there to welcome the individual back from his or her thinking time. Others mention that deadlines, challenges and pressure also help them to be creative:

I am most innovative when I am travelling in the car, walking in the countryside, in the bath, just before bed/first thing in the morning, usually those times when we sort of half switch-off. I am also very creative when I can bounce off others who are inspirational and innovative too. At those times the environment isn't that important because we sort of get caught up in the ideas and don't notice.

Creativity is not limited to 9–5. A *variety* of conditions, it could vary from being under pressure to after lunch dozing, it's that half-conscious connection with a near dream like state that ideas can flow. Walking also helps.

On a hillside overlooking the whole of Portsmouth, the Solent and the Isle of Wight, with a picnic, my bike and a glass or two of wine! So bottom line answer: where all my senses are being tickled but especially ambience, sound, visual, etc.

Their sources of inspiration were equally varied:

Anything new, a place I haven't seen before, a picture on a card/postcard, a quote I haven't heard before, lyrics in songs, videos, stories in books/ magazine articles, driving with nothing on my mind and suddenly a thought comes in that is somehow everything I have been waiting for but didn't know it.

Events, other people, but mostly 'voices' in my head!

Books, pictures, images, songs, landscapes, memories, connections, others.

Thinking time and believing anything is possible.

Aesthetics, nature, music, people.

Inspirational moments in life, this may either be something in nature, music, something I've read, an actual event. I think this mainly relates to situations in which I see the hidden strength, the focus of conviction, beating the odds, excelling in all these types of things.

If you expose yourself to richness of experience you can stimulate your creativity by drawing down from external stimuli and other pleasurable experiences. However well motivated you are there may be times when you need to recharge, or to be inspired to enable you to work more effectively with others. When you find that your creativity is being stifled, take a break and do something completely different. Take regular time out to indulge yourself, use others for support, and bounce around ideas however crazy, build on initial fleeting thoughts to anchor more tangible concepts. Unlearn lessons from childhood: say 'I can' instead of 'I can't'. Tune into your surroundings by being inspired by a view, music, and space. Some people find that they need a special environment to be creative: this may be a special place, a desk, or a room at home that becomes the focus for their thinking time. Other people go running, or take part in some other kind of physical activity. People who undertake a lot of travelling try to utilize this potentially 'dead' time to organize their thoughts.

Stages of creativity

Paul E Torrance founded the creativity movement in education. He focused on developing children's problem solving abilities. This he believed supported the child's unique authenticity, his or her spirit. He defines creativity as:

Fluency: thinking of many ideas.
Flexibility: thinking of different ways to do, or use, things.
Originality: thinking of different unique things.
Elaboration: thinking of details and embellishments to an idea.

He states that it takes courage to be creative: 'Just as soon as you have an idea you are in a minority of one.'

Robinson and Stern, writing in *Corporate Creativity*, suggest there are four strategies that companies can use to promote diverse stimuli:

1. Identify stimuli and provide them to employees.

2. Rotate employees into every job that they are capable of doing.

3. Arrange for employees to interact with those outside the company who are likely to be the source of stimuli.

4. Create opportunities for employees to bring into the organization stimuli they get on their own.

A stimulus can either push someone in a completely new direction or give that person fresh insight into what he or she has already set out to do.

They also state that what serves as a powerful stimulus for one person, for whatever reason may not even be noticed by someone else. One of their most important findings was that they believed that rather than focusing on devising and delivering stimuli to a select few employees outside of their normal work, it is more important for a company to recognize that most stimuli that lead to creative acts will be found by the employees themselves, and when they are it is important that they should have the opportunity to bring these stimuli into the organization and put them to use.

All the best customer focused organizations encourage individuals to take the initiative, to respond positively to challenge and to recognize the very real threat posed by competitors. Those who adopt a 'me too' philosophy will always be the ones who are in the slipstream of others.

Creating the 'right' environment, however, can be more of a challenge. Lack of understanding about the process of innovation has traditionally led to people dividing themselves into two camps: those who are seen as creative and those who are not. This applies to individuals' assessments of themselves as well as the perceptions of others. By recognizing how the process of innovation works individuals and teams can develop a clearer understanding and respect for each other's contribution.

One model that you will see used in many contexts to describe the act of creativity is the one suggested by Joseph Wallas in 1926:

■ *Preparation:* researching, data-gathering, primarily factual, you may have a idea of an area worth exploring, but it is unconfirmed, it may be nothing more than a 'hunch' or feeling.

- *Incubation:* the ideas are beginning to form, but we let them simmer, we leave them at the back of our minds while we are doing other things, we bring them forward from time to time but we are not ready to act on them.

- *Illumination:* this is the reason why a light bulb is often used to symbolize idea generation, or creativity, it is that stage or moment when you realize that you know what it all means or why you have spent so long thinking about something; it is often described as the 'aha' moment.

- *Verification:* this is the checking out period, talking to others, sharing the idea, refining it, qualifying it, making sure that it really is worth investing time and resources in taking it forward into the next stage.

Other writers, including Goleman, have made reference to the work of Jules Henri Poincaré and others in developing this model to include other stages, notably *execution*. This is another important stage and it may sound the death knell for many ideas, as it takes a different set of behaviours and often requires the inventor to have to communicate and collaborate with others.

The importance of understanding innovation and creativity does not just apply to creating blended learning solutions: it has a huge importance at the very core of how organizations compete effectively in their markets and in the recruitment and retention of key talent.

> The emotional foundation of the innovator at work is taking pleasure in originality. Creativity on the job revolves around applying new ideas to achieve results. People who have this knack can quickly identify key issues and simplify problems that seem overwhelmingly complex. Most important they can find original connections and patterns that others overlook. People who lack a flair for innovation, by contrast, typically miss the larger picture and get enmeshed in details, and so deal with problems only slowly, even tediously. Their fear of risk makes them shy away from novel ideas. And when they try to find solutions, they often fail to realize that what worked in the past is not always the answer for the future. . . People who are uncomfortable with risk become critics and nay-sayers. Defensive and cautious, they may constantly deride or undermine innovative ideas. (Goleman, *Working with Emotional Intelligence*)

As Goleman illustrates above, one of the biggest frustrations for creative people is the need to justify their ideas to others, not just through a bureaucratic process, but more often as a result of the fear or uncertainty of others. This often gives rise to the cry, 'Fools, can't you see?' Ultimately, people often just walk away, because they despair of the doubts and questions raised by those who are risk-adverse.

When you are creating learning experiences for others take time to help them explore their own creativity; use a variety of sources to help them recognize the rich variety and ways of doing things differently.

TOOLS AND TECHNIQUES

There are a number of tools and techniques that can help the creative process and you are likely to find a role for all of them as you work through the process of creating and implementing blended learning solutions.

Pure creative thinking is often fast: the speed of creative thought is frightening in terms of speed and complexity, because when your mind is flowing it is almost the equivalent of a mental meltdown. On a particularly good day the senses collide, hearing, seeing, feeling, sensing. Capturing this, you can share the information with others. Techniques like mind mapping help in allowing the thoughts to be captured on one page, with the inter-connections.

You may find tools and techniques like Buzan's Mind Mapping®, de Bono's Six Thinking Hats or brainstorming help you to focus, but if you have the ability to be creative all you really need is a means of recording, because when you find yourself in a creative state it is a force that cannot really be controlled, it has an energy and speed all of its own. Equally it can disappear at will, but the good news is that it will return often when you least expect it, nudging at the corners of your mind, saying, 'Remember me?'

Visualization

Visualization is a very powerful tool in helping individuals to see alternatives; however, some will need a lot of support to realize its potential. Remember the saying, 'If you keep on doing what you always did, you always get what you always got'? Creating blended learning is about enabling people to see alternatives so that they don't always get what they always got. Achieving this shift in perspective will take time. Helping the individual to take small incremental steps towards another vision should ultimately lead to them having another view on the world. Companies like Disney use a technique called 'displayed thinking' where ideas are incubated by a continuous process of brainstorming when the originators of the ideas allow others to add their input.

Creative problem solving

For many people it is helping them to identify alternatives, offering support as they work through options. Often the issue simply seems too big a challenge. Helping them to identify the issue and break it down into manageable chunks is an important first step. Then they can move forward using steps like these:

- identify the problem;
- think around it;
- seek the involvement and views of interested people with differing views;
- isolate the problem and pay attention to it;
- use a variety of problem solving techniques;
- think around the problem and explore all ideas and options;
- focus on solutions in a structured way;
- agree an action plan for implementation;
- review and evaluate the outcomes.

Again, working in teams can broaden the perspectives and create different solutions.

If you are working as a team to create blended learning it is important that you help explore all the options open to you, but also help each other to open your eyes so that you see things that you normally might ignore. Encourage each other to be curious, to have an openness and desire to find out more. In today's society more than ever before, there is a critical need for knowledge management. The advent of the Internet and the speed of technological development makes it essential to have some kind of mechanism to help you sift and identify what is important and relevant and what to ignore. Just like the saying, 'You don't know what you don't know' you can waste vast amounts of time searching for what you think you might find.

Storyboards/flowcharts

When designing learning events that involve a technological application there is often a need to create flowcharts or storyboards that act as a route map showing the key stages and the progression through the learning. There are also authoring tools that are being developed all the time. The key function of the tool or technique is to ensure that where appropriate the logical sequence of the learning is captured. Like any journey, there may also be stopping off points where the learner will be encouraged to ask for guidance, or to explore concepts along the way, but it is important that an overall map exists. This will relate to a bigger site plan if you are creating an ambitious internal learning environment, or just the key stages on a particular journey.

In practical terms a flowchart, storyboard, or map can not only be used to explain the flow and key steps to Web designers or other multimedia producers, it can also be used as a visual tool to illustrate the route map of the overall development. The need to strip out irrelevant information and define the key steps is a valuable learning lesson for everyone. Taking simple straightforward steps in a learning process is one of the key benefits of online learning. Achieving the fluency, when designers want to take you to a level of detail that trainers may take as a given in their trainer notes, may initially seem challenging, but in online learning no assumptions can be made: it has to be defined with absolute clarity.

DESIGNING AND WRITING ONLINE LEARNING

The principles behind designing online learning are the same as for any other learning intervention. As highlighted in Chapters 2 and 3, everyone has particular preferences when learning, and in designing the learning experience it is important to take account of these preferences and build a learning experience that provides enough variety to cater for them. The very nature of how we learn means that online learning can only ever be one part of a broader learning experience. Thinking creatively about the design, however, can mean that it can be stimulating, interesting and intimate for the learner.

Your role in the design may be more hands-off unless you have developed particular expertise in Web design, but you can influence and give valuable feedback to the designers on the overall look and feel. As highlighted in Chapter 2 and the case studies, finding providers who are prepared to work closely with you is a very important part of the process. Equally important is the recognition of where your own skills lie. If we look at the various stages in the design process (see Chapter 3) it will be possible to see that there are a number of key steps in the creation of learning materials and you should be able to identify where your own preferences and expertise lies.

Who should be designing the materials?

One really important consideration is how to develop the materials. Although it may be challenging and interesting to develop Web design skills in order to develop your own online materials, it may not be practical or possible within your timeframe of introducing blended learning. There are a number of roles that you can valuably perform in the process, but unlike some of the other roles, writing for the Web is more specialized, and you must ask yourself if this is the best use of your time.

Guardians of intellectual property

One way of achieving a best fit is to recognize the roles and expertise involved in the total process. Internally it may be more appropriate for you to become a guardian of intellectual property (see the Diageo case study), recognizing your breadth and depth of knowledge about content, the users/learners and the learning and development process. Externally there may be Web designers and authors. By taking the expertise from the right people with the right knowledge it will be far easier to create a blended solution that has a higher chance of success.

One of the interesting issues for creative individuals and the new breed of knowledge workers is how to protect intellectual property. In *Intellectual Property: A business guide* (CBI and KPMG) there is a useful article by Eastwood and Zair examining how companies can seek to be proactive about their IP assets. They suggest that there are a range of questions that CEOs should ask themselves; one of the most critical is an analysis of what IP assets exist in the organization, where they are held and how they are protected. They suggest that very few organizations will be able to answer these questions with any degree of certainty.

Recording and protecting what you know

To protect your intellectual property it is absolutely vital to keep meticulous records of all the stages in development. One of the major issues is disclosure. You can sign confidentiality agreements and non-disclosure documents, but it is important to assess the level of risk you are taking when you start talking about your ideas and concepts. The best advice is to be careful, recognize the value of what you have created and take professional advice where appropriate.

Auditing content

Auditing and identifying where relevant content is located within an organization is also highly relevant. Benchmarking best practice externally and networking with fellow professionals is another important role.

Assembling a team of sample users to pilot and test the material will be a major contribution to the final success of the product. Equally, introducing the concept of blended learning to colleagues and to the rest of the organization can help to ensure that the implementation is more successful.

Design principles

What the online component of blended learning shouldn't be is a training programme simply put onto the Web. Used properly there are excellent opportunities to make learning interactive, dynamic and fun, but it does require the use of specialist design software and IT skills to create an effective learning environment.

There are some important criteria to remember when developing online learning (you can use this as a checklist for evaluating material developed by others):

■ content should be high quality and interesting;

■ less equals more: remember your learner will potentially be reading off a screen;

■ think about print options: some information can be printed off to read rather than scrolling through a screen;

■ use a journalistic, conversational style rather than an academic approach;

■ you can refer people to other sites for articles, resources;

■ ideally use a designer to enhance your words on screen;

■ recognize that many people may be viewing your material on laptops or smaller screens;

■ make careful use of illustrations and animation;

■ remember that unlike some other forms of learning where the sequence may be more controlled, an online learner may be entering a screen in a more random sequence. They may also drill down, so having clear forms of navigation will be important to help the learners find their way around.

Like the early days of video when people were coming to terms with the ability to photograph people moving, recognize the reason why you are using online learning. It should be giving the learner a richer experience than simply reading flat text. If all you put up on the Web is text, however well created, you need to ask whether this is the best way of presenting your information. Equally, if you create space that is over-full with animation or illustrations your learner may simply find it a distraction.

CONTRACT WITH THE LEARNER

One of the benefits of an online environment is that it can create an intimacy with the learner, which needs to be respected. One of the issues with e-commerce has been a very natural reluctance on the part of the user to give personal information when undertaking a transaction, and learning is no different. Once users have started a process of interaction they will be revealing information about themselves, which should be protected and treated with integrity. The very nature of the learning that they may be undertaking may include them recording their personal responses to different situations, they may be carrying out assessments, they may be sharing their views with others. The following checklist highlights some key areas.

Checklist

Does the learning environment that we have created:

- treat the learner with respect, clarifying what information is confidential and what may be shared with other users, for example surveys, norm data, shared discussions?

- seek to engage the learner in an experience that is relevant, inspiring, fun and different?

- encourage learners to take responsibility for their own learning through carefully planned stages of developing personal ownership?

■ provide learning experiences that are stimulating, interesting and use the right medium for the learning, rather than technology for its own sake?

■ use language that is jargon-free, clear and engaging for the learner?

■ make the connections between offline and online learning and the working environment, so that the learner is able to put the learning into practice?

■ provide opportunities for assessment that are valid, reliable and meaningful?

■ build opportunities and capacity for online discussion with others in a safe and secure environment?

■ encourage the learner to take action and invite feedback from their peers and managers?

■ offer the right level of support through prompt helpdesk technical support, one-to-one coaching, as appropriate?

Implementation checklist

■ Have we raised awareness of the learning potential?

■ Have we planned the launch of blended learning with the right level of technical and offline support to help with the first few weeks of implementation?

■ Have we tested or run a pilot of the materials?

USING OTHER MEDIA

As well as online learning there may be other elements of learning that need designing and the same principles apply whether it is a CD ROM, video-streaming, distance or open learning: the focus must always be on the end user. Some questions to ask yourself and the designers when commissioning any form of learning are, is this the most effective way of transmitting the learning to the end user? Is it interesting? Does it take the right amount of time? Is the learning reinforced in different ways? Increasingly standards are being set, such as SCORM or IMS (see definitions in Chapter 1), so there is another set of questions to ensure compliance with global standards.

OTHER KEY POINTS TO REMEMBER

One of the disadvantages with the growth of more technology-based learning is the lack of human contact: individual learners are losing the opportunity to talk through their embryonic ideas with other people. The whole philosophy of self-managed learning provides individuals with choices about how and where they learn, which has distinct advantages for both the individual and the organization. However, one of the potential losses from the reduction in training programmes is not so much what happens in the classroom or lecture theatre, but the learning that takes place on training events in those quieter, more intimate moments when two people start talking to each other at the end of a day, or in seminar groups before someone interrupts you and tells you to get on with the task. Therefore, when introducing blended learning it is important to remember the need to include opportunities for this level of personal contact to still form part of the learning experience.

Working virtually

One of the distinct advantages of technology is the ability to transmit messages rapidly around the world. One way that this can help in the design of learning is that designers do not need to be in the same location. The speed of communication can also help more locally. As mentioned above, Disney uses a technique called 'displayed thinking', where projects that are being worked on are literally displayed on the wall. This allows people working in different areas to add their own suggestions, and it serves as a valuable communication tool. This same process can be used to share information with others using email or company Intranets. Using techniques such as mind mapping or sticky notes can transmit a lot of information simply. There are a number of advantages to this approach:

1. It allows for the natural and creative development of ideas.

2. A number of people can contribute at the same time.

3. Using simple techniques, ideas can be commented upon, amended, or added to, while retaining the original document.

4. It is possible to work across different time zones and shorten the development time.

5. Working in this way can help to forge global links and overcome cultural differences.

6. Everyone can work at a time, place and pace to suit their preferred learning styles.

7. To be successful designers need to follow the same principles, as mentioned above.

8. The same disciplines of meeting deadlines and responsiveness also need to apply in this virtual environment.

E-technologies have particular relevance in supporting virtual teams. This can involve you as part of a global team, or working with teams that are working virtually. With virtual teams it is important to establish the ground rules for working together, including the following:

■ identify what technology support is available and how to make best use of it;

■ agree the frequency of meetings;

■ commitment to attendance, on time and uninterrupted;

■ agree team rules such as responding to emails within certain time-frames;

■ establish ways of using time efficiently, eg defining the purpose of virtual meetings;

■ use other methods to share information, for example circulate material prior to a meeting so that everyone comes prepared to contribute;

■ ideally, from time to time get together in person to form more substantial relationships;

■ understand each team member's expectations and needs when working virtually;

■ constantly reassess the opportunities for extending the technology support as systems improve, but use it appropriately; do not use valuable conference air time on something that should have been emailed.

By using this checklist you have the opportunity to exploit the advantages and minimize the disadvantages of working virtually.

5

Tracking blended learning

INVITING FEEDBACK

Who gives you feedback? Do you invite it? Do you believe it? As professionals, we should be able to ask for feedback and absorb it into our ongoing development. Unfortunately there are very few people who are really skilled at giving it. If you are training people to assess or coach, you will recognize the importance of doing it properly, but many people give feedback that is unhelpful during appraisals or performance management sessions. With less opportunity for training, there are ever more instances of unskilled feedback.

If you do develop a clear understanding of your strengths, you are better able to help people give you feedback. By asking the right questions, you will be able to elicit information about your own performance. If you develop experience as a communicator you will also be able to identify other people's responses to you. Feedback can be considered in a number of contexts:

- How effective am I at giving feedback? How do I know? How could I check my understanding?

- Do I ask for feedback? If yes, with what result? If no, what positive actions can I take to overcome this?

- Who do I really trust to help me explore the areas where I feel less confident?

- How can I enhance my skills in giving feedback?

- What would I like to do differently when giving feedback?

These questions are intended as prompts for you to consider, but as part of your personal development you may want to explore these in more depth with your own personal coach or mentor.

REFLECTING ON LEARNING

Ask yourself and your learners the following questions:

- Have I created the right place for me to learn?

- Do I take responsibility for my learning?

- Do I use my preferred learning styles?

- Can I learn despite poor teaching? Do I seek additional coaching?

- Am I actively involved in the learning process?

- Can I learn in many different ways; do I know what I need to memorize, what I need to understand and what I need to learn by doing?

- Do I seek feedback on my learning, on my performance?

- Do I learn from my mistakes?

- Do I regularly take a break and do something else to energize me?

- Do I share and celebrate my successes in learning?

An important part of your learning is to help your learners to review the outcomes of their development activities. Encourage them to ask themselves the following after a learning event:

- What went well? Why?

- What could have gone better? Why?

- How could I improve next time?

- What have I learnt?

- How will I use this learning in the future?

Implementing a blended learning initiative should be no different to any other learning and development provision. One of the first steps will be to identify with the sponsor the particular learning need so that at a later stage it can be tailored to the learners. There are many ways in which you can undertake this, however it is important to remember to also set it in the context of a business needs analysis. If the organization is aligned then the two should link synergistically from an individual and organizational perspective. Given the changing nature and culture of organizations, describing the activity that you undertake as a training needs analysis (TNA) may not be appropriate in all cases, particularly as training may not be the only solution. However, for the purposes of this analysis the term will be used in its broadest sense.

In undertaking a TNA or identifying any learning and development intervention there are a number of key steps (the detail of this process is outlined in Chapter 3):

1. Responding to the request for an intervention from a client/sponsor.

2. Aligning the proposal with the overall business objectives: ultimately any investment in learning and development should be matched to the needs of the business.

3. Designing and developing the solutions, including analysing the opportunity for blended learning.

4. Delivering a solution that meets the special learning needs of an individual or team.

5. Tracking and reviewing the progress of the intervention.

6. Monitoring and learning from the outcomes.

In order to design the right learning experience the developer should identify with the client the strategic overview, the business objectives and the required outcomes from the training. Once you are in direct contact with the learners you should also be able to respond to their individual needs within the context of the overall desired outcomes.

Despite advances in learning interventions there are still many examples of individuals being 'sent' on training programmes without any assessment of the real learning need. This is particularly true in organizations that operate menus of training and development. If you are trying to suggest that a blended learning solution might be appropriate, the questions asked and the research undertaken can make all the difference. It can also have a tremendous impact not only on the resources invested but also the strategic outcomes, which is why it is so important to undertake a TNA effectively.

You may be in a 'start-up' position in a new organization or function; you may have just joined an organization with a specific objective to develop a training function or provision. You may be an external provider invited to work in partnership with an organization. Whatever your role you need to be able to help the organization, client, or individual to articulate their needs.

One way of helping clients to focus on their needs is to ask, 'At the end of the training or learning process, what would you like people to be able to do that they cannot do now, or what would you like to be different?' By helping people to think about the future you begin to identify the start of their journey. If it is a significant training or development need you may need to undertake your analysis at a number of levels within the organization. Within this process you may find it helpful to consider the following:

- Identify client/corporate goals/desired outcomes.

- What are the specific business objectives linked to this need?

- How will the development meet those needs?

- What training or learning intervention has already taken place?

- What is working well that we can build on?

- What needs to be developed, improved?

- What new skills, competencies are required?

- Who needs to attend?

- Who will endorse/sponsor the learning and development?

- How will you evaluate/measure the effectiveness of the training?

- What information is available about the participants – what do you perceive to be their needs?

Once you have gathered this information you will be in a better position to make an assessment of what could be offered and how the different components could be combined into an overall solution.

Another key aspect will be the financial implications of any intervention and at a time of reducing budgets it will be important to prioritize development needs. One of the criticisms often levelled at learning and development functions is their inability to evaluate the effectiveness of any learning and development intervention and to identify the proposed return on investment, often because it is seen to be developing 'soft' skills. Tracking blended learning should be no different and in many ways more important. One of the first actions should be to identify what mechanisms are currently in place to measure the effectiveness of any solution. In today's learning environment many organizations are questioning their investment in learning and development. At times of cost reduction a learning and development function can look an easy target.

Every part of an organization including learning and development should always be examining their contribution to the bottom line. The effectiveness with which you conduct the analysis of training needs is critical to the eventual success of your training event. If you miss vital clues in establishing what your client or participants need to learn, the outcomes will not maximize your training intervention/impact. However effective your design, delivery or evaluation if you have not clearly identified the needs you are potentially wasting your and, more unfortunately, your client/participants' time.

However you first become involved in a TNA, you will normally find that there is an underlying need to do something different. Often clients will ask you to provide a solution without necessarily clearly articulating what the need is; it may be described as a problem or an issue or something that needs to be changed. There can be a variety of reasons for the need for change, some of which are:

■ business performance not up to expectation;

■ new legislation;

■ professional or personal development needs;

■ customer complaints rising;

■ staffing issues such as poor morale, high turnover of staff;

■ the need to move into new markets or develop new products.

Whatever the reason, you need to establish what that real need is before you can start to suggest fully effective solutions. This can sometimes require a certain amount of resilience on your part in asking some difficult and probing questions in areas that clients and participants may initially be reluctant to discuss. Equally, they genuinely may not be able to clearly articulate the needs because they are too close to the issues. In these situations your skills as a consultant/facilitator will need to be particularly sharp. If you are suggesting a blended learning solution you may also have to overcome a level of resistance, not only from the sponsor but also from the individuals, simply because they may not be familiar with the online learning components. In suggesting a blended learning solution it will be important to be able to demonstrate how it works and how the different components fit together.

WHAT ARE THE ESSENTIAL ELEMENTS OF A TNA?

First, there has to be a need and the learning solution should be seen in the context of what the organization is trying to achieve. A further key element is to establish the gap that needs to bridged between performance now and the performance in the future. This gap may need more than one step before it is bridged. In making judgements about the size of the gap you will need to take measurements. The techniques used in researching the problem need to be designed to provide the information you require.

In conducting your analysis it is worth keeping in mind the fact that not all solutions necessarily involve training. Having established the need for a TNA there are a number of research techniques at your disposal, including:

■ observation;

■ interviews;

■ questionnaires;

■ critical incident diaries;

■ repertory grid;

■ assessments.

Cost-effectiveness

There is always a dilemma in deciding how much information you need to collect. Only experience will tell you whether you get it right, but examining your methods will accelerate that learning process. A retrospective view of the TNA strategy against the evaluation data will tell you whether you:

■ missed context issues;

■ attempted to train the already competent;

■ understood the desired outcomes;

■ improved the organization's performance;

■ (bottom line) met the success criteria agreed with the client prior to starting the project.

At all times you need to keep the key stakeholders' outcomes in mind, avoiding being over-elaborate and presenting a solution looking for a problem. You run the risk of losing credibility if you suggest solutions that do not match your research findings. The 'Here is one I did earlier' syndrome may suit some organizations looking for a tried and tested solution to a generic problem, but most organizations who are willing to fund a TNA expect the eventual solution to be tailored to their organization, rather than trying to fit a ready-made solution to their needs.

If you are thinking as a strategic partner then it will be important to present the findings of the TNA professionally to your client. The results of the TNA may be presented initially to your client sponsor who may then want you, either on your own or with them, to present the findings and your proposals for the next steps to senior management. A presentation provides you with an opportunity to gauge reactions, such as:

- Have I got them on board?
- Am I using the right language?
- Have I matched their expectations?
- Do I need to conduct further study?
- Will they trust me to work with their employees with this training solution?

Sometimes when presenting research data, you may come across organizations and managers who believe they know the solution before you start. They effectively have the report written and are looking for you to provide the supporting evidence. Professionally you need to be very aware of the expectations of your sponsor, but it is important to present unbiased findings.

Evaluation plays a part in providing essential information that the event is on track and is achieving its overall aims. A process of evaluation should be built in throughout the training process and you should be looking all the time for opportunities to obtain feedback on your effectiveness. Although the primary role of your evaluation approach is to give key stakeholders information, this should not prevent you using any data-gathering systems to provide information on your performance.

As a guideline you should always consider your own 'brand' and ask yourself, 'Is this activity, are these findings presented in a way that reflects my professionalism and my integrity?' The process for undertaking the evaluation should be built in at the start of the training cycle.

Unless success criteria are established it makes evaluation at the end of the event more difficult and probably less focused. The effective developer will ensure that clear success criteria are established and agreed with key stakeholders and clients. These will need to be anchored in the research findings of the TNA.

A key question in the process is, 'Did I set benchmarks against which to judge the level of performance?' If the purpose of training is to help close the gap between actual and desired performance you must be able to define what that original level of performance was.

During the designing stage it is important to construct cost-effective solutions to bridge the training gap. Part of that construction requires checks and balances to be included that will allow fine adjustments to be made to keep the training on course to deliver the desired outcomes. In examining your evaluation strategy you will need to ask yourself whether these checks and balances were enough.

On the assumption that the design broadly reflects the TNA research data it will be useful to examine any flexibility you introduced and whether it was sufficient. Unless your training event is designed to follow a rigid script, your participants are not likely to detect any variations. These variations are not necessarily related to a design flaw but reflect the fact that participants have different learning styles and come to events with various experiences. In the design stage the effective trainer will include possible variations. Sometimes these are not written formally into a training brief but are mental or personal notes. With a blended solution these variations will have to be analysed and where appropriate written into the storyboard/flowchart content.

Whenever you implement these variations you will be making a judgement about their effectiveness. In order to put these into perspective it will be necessary to seek the views of others. If you are running a number of events this can be done by constructing an evaluation approach that allows you to compare reactions to the session in question with one without the variations. This will be particularly important if you are seeking to introduce a different approach through the use of blended learning.

Another key indicator might be how quickly it was possible to get a learning point across. If the event is a one-off, comparison is obviously not possible. In this case you can elicit feedback by asking direct questions either during or immediately after the session in which you introduced the variation. It is worth keeping in mind that this level of evaluation is not necessarily for your key stakeholders, but is for you to gather information about your own effectiveness.

USING A LEARNING MANAGEMENT SYSTEM

Something that can help you manage the underpinning data-gathering is an LMS.

An LMS also provides the technology infrastructure for companies to manage human capital development by tracking employee training information and managing, tracking and launching all events and resources associated with corporate learning. A Web-based LMS provides online course and event management, content and resource management, comprehensive assessments, enhanced skills gap analysis, content authoring, email notifications, and real-time integration with human resource, financial and ERP systems. An LMS manages all training delivery types – third party and internal – including classroom-based, e-learning, virtual classroom, technology-based training, books and video. An LMS also provides access to authoring tools, 360-degree assessments, learning content management, and/or virtual classroom functionality. See the THINQ case study in Chapter 6.

OVERCOMING OBSTACLES

Despite the positive potential of blended learning there are still sceptics, particularly of the online components. Everything we know about learning focuses on the importance of recognizing the needs of the learner. To overcome resistance it is important to understand the issues. Think about the following question:

What gets in the way of your learning?

- Time?
- Work pressure?

- Inertia?

- Motivation?

- Commitments to others?

Sometimes it is a combination of factors: wrong time, wrong place, wrong people. Think about your own learning preferences: how could you create an environment that worked for you? These are some very real factors that get in the way of learning, some of which are illustrated in more detail in the case studies (see Chapter 6). If you are looking to create an effective learning environment it is critical to incorporate what we know about how people learn (see Chapter 2).

One of the other potential obstacles is a reluctance to move away from classroom activity, and it is important to acknowledge and recognize the value of what happens in the classroom or workshop environment. This is highlighted in the following comment by Professor Joel Podolny, Professor of Organizational Behaviour and Strategic Management at Stanford, quoted in an article by Della Bradshaw in the *Financial Times*, 24 June 2002: 'One of the things I have been increasingly struck by is how much in the classroom there is a subtext going on which is unrelated to the content.' Social interaction and verbal jousting are the sorts of things he believes are missing even in the best pure e-learning courses. 'It is a very dry unmotivating experience,' he suggests. He is not alone: in the research for this book others have expressed similar views. The impact of such comments is that others hear them and even without trying it decide that e-learning is not for them. The very real challenge for e-learning designers is how to create learning experiences that are innovative and stimulating and which complement other, more traditional forms of learning.

AREAS TO CONSIDER

Learning in front of a computer screen can be seen as a solitary experience, and people can switch off mentally if they are not stimulated by what they see on the screen. Factually correct content does not necessarily mean a good learning experience. It is the method of learning, the design and other methods that keep the learner interested.

> If you teach via a screen you do not have that human interaction, so you have to assume that the user is getting bored all the time. Companies go out of their way to choose a trainer who can present in an engaging and valuable way, then they are evaluated at the end of the course. With e-learning it is the other way around. (Jan Hagen, Widelearning.com, quoted in an article by John Robinson, E-learning Supplement, *Personnel Today*, 27 March 2001)

In this context critics of e-learning doubt whether the technique offers anything in the way of a learning experience for learners. They argue that technology is dictating the way individuals learn rather than supporting the educational process. Other issues include learners missing the interpersonal contact with others and being nervous about the technology. It can also be quite challenging to be sitting at your desk and ignoring interruptions, trying to focus on learning.

However, balanced against this are many other benefits for the learner including not having to stay away from home, less travel and, if tailored properly, learning that is really focused on the learner.

If blended learning has any hope of success we need to take account of the very real reservations that people have and to work to overcome this resistance. This will be achieved by creating inspiring and stimulating experiences that are not judged as being so by the learning designers but by the end users themselves.

As a final point, here's a reprise of the comment made by one of our case study contributors:

> Above all remember the need to remain focused on the learner. Perhaps the biggest danger in any 'e' or blended solution project is becoming focused on technology/creativity, and not the audience. It is important that the learners' needs are fully captured and documented at the start of the project and that any success measures are based around these.

6
Case studies

Rolls-Royce plc
Diageo plc
DaimlerChrysler UK Ltd
Avis Europe plc
Ashridge
Basic Skills Agency
Computeach International
CNDL Group
Nationwide Trust
The US Department of Health and Human Services
THINQ Limited

ROLLS-ROYCE PLC

Rolls-Royce plc is a global company providing power for land, sea and air. The company has established a balanced business, with leading positions in civil aerospace, defence aerospace, marine and energy markets, where its core technology can be applied over a broad range of products and services.

Its aerospace businesses have customers in over 150 countries, including more than 500 airlines, 2,400 corporate and utility operators and 160 armed forces, using both fixed and rotary wing aircraft.

Rolls-Royce is the global leader in marine power systems, with a broad product range and full systems integration capability. More than 2,000 commercial marine customers and over 30 navies use Rolls-Royce propulsion and products. In energy markets, the company is investing in new products and capabilities for the oil and gas industry and power generation.

Rolls-Royce pioneered gas turbine technology for aerospace, power generation and marine propulsion, and is involved in major future programmes in these fields, including the WR-21 marine engine, leading-edge water jet propulsion systems, and combat engines for Eurofighter Typhoon and the Joint Strike Fighter.

What examples do you have of blended learning?

ERP training programmes – an example of blended learning applied within Rolls-Royce plc

Since 2000, Rolls-Royce plc has been faced with training requirements to support a large Enterprise Resource Planning (ERP) implementation, involving major changes to company processes and the introduction of SAP as the IT system to support the processes.

Over the last two years, training has been required to be delivered to over 10,000 people in 70 different roles in the UK, USA and Germany, covering 15 major sites and 15 separate business units. The approach has been:

■ a communication cascade to inform and prepare people for the change, and to engage people from each business early in the process to deliver the communications;

■ initial 'generic' training via computer-based training as a prerequisite to instructor-led sessions;

■ role-based instructor-led training on the new processes and system transactions to support the process;

■ support via local 'super users' using a 'training environment' on the SAP system, supported by reusing training lessons delivered online and paper-based materials (eg quick reference guides).

Using this model training was delivered to 6,000 people in 2000/2001, and a similar model is being used for the roll-out of the new HR system in 2001/2002 to 24,000 people.

What were the biggest challenges in setting them up?

Not all went smoothly – the major issues were:

■ Couldn't secure release of personnel from the businesses early enough or in sufficient quantity to follow through the plan in its entirety.

■ Focus was on personnel whose role was changing. After implementation, the main blockers to success were the people communicating with these people, and their line management, so that they were able to perform effectively in their new roles.

■ People generally not comfortable with the idea of learning online – felt remote and unsupported, so pressure was on to deliver as much as possible in instructor-led mode.

■ Not enough time was available to people after being trained to embed the learning in the training environment before implementation.

How did you overcome them?

Some re-planning of training was required to ensure that the essentials were trained before go-live, with top-up training after implementation, to make best use of the available training resource.

Post-implementation communication events were held from senior level downwards to reinforce the changes required to embed the new processes.

Evaluation of the feedback of the online learning led to the conclusion that the material itself was not the issue, but its accessibility and the way it was communicated. The material is now better structured and being made available via the company Intranet (rather than via network drives). The online learning was most successful in businesses where the instructor-led training did not go over the introductory online learning lessons in the classroom (thus providing an incentive to complete them), but reinforced those lessons, used the face-to-face element largely as a vehicle for communicating change, and introduced the transaction-level online learning lessons so that delegates were well prepared for learning in this way post-workshop.

What have been the benefits?

The successful outcomes have been:

■ A large body of training materials that can be made available to users to support the system post-implementation – supported by a central team ensuring this is updated in line with system changes.

■ The system is live and operating.

■ Some of the benefit stream is now being realized.

■ People encouraged to use the company Intranet as their 'one-stop shop' for finding out about training.

What advice would you give to others?

Don't underestimate the attachment many people feel to 'classroom' training. There were many messages being transmitted by the workshop leaders and training coordinators that the online training was 'second-best' – most of this sub-consciously. Examples of the language used were:

> 'Sorry we can't use the proper system for this – we'll have to use this lesson instead.'

> 'I don't know why the lesson does that – it's not very good is it.' This example was a lesson to go through a transaction in the HR system to update a personal address. The lesson forced the use of proper address format – eg initial capital letters, use of post code – not to reflect the system (the address was free-form text in reality), but to reinforce the fact that the system used this directly to post out pay slips, so the format had to be correct.

I think we missed a stage of getting the training deliverers bought in to the training delivery methodology, so that they were giving positive messages about all parts of the training.

What next?

We are working with one business to move their 'people processes' and associated use of SAP from the HR team to line managers. This will involve a more heavily integrated set of workshops/process training/transaction training sessions, which will be a mix of instructor-led and online.

For further information contact: brian.hayer@rolls-royce.com.

DIAGEO PLC

Diageo is the world's leading premium drinks business operating in 180 countries and with a turnover of over £11 billion (2002). Global Supply employs some 10,000 people, and is responsible for the production, packaging and distribution of Diageo beers, wines and spirits worldwide. Key brands include Guinness, Baileys, Smirnoff, Johnnie Walker and Captain Morgan.

What examples do you have of blended learning?

One example of blended learning is in the support we placed around the delivery of a High Performance Coaching (HPC) workshop. Initially the two-day classroom-based workshop was targeted across Diageo Global Supply's management population. The workshop has four areas of pre-work (nominating a coaching target, conducting 360-degree feedback, identifying a key performance area, and identifying a personal development area that would benefit from coaching). Moving forward, the workshop will be rolled out in different ways to further levels of the organization with the e-learning element seen to complement the learning process.

The e-learning part of HPC for Diageo Global Supply was one of our first ventures into the use of e-learning and blended learning. We did not decide to reduce the time on the two-day workshop as a return on investment argument. This was really seen as an enhancement of the workshop and positioning it as a programme rather than an event. It also meant that we hoped to really delve down into the content of the coaching models and take out all reference to detailed explanations of theories on slides at the workshop.

This was the principle we defined:

Provide blended learning to HPC via e-learning application prior to attending the facilitator-led workshop in order to increase content knowledge and increase the practice and consolidation of learning at the two-day workshop.

The scope of the blended learning was communicated to stakeholders as:

HPC Blended Learning. . .

Is:

■ Tool to engage Global Supply participants pre-programme.

■ Tracks completion of pre-work.

■ Covers theory/content to provide more practice and coaching opportunities at the programme.

■ Participants arrive on the programme with a common knowledge base.

■ Provides Global Supply with standards applied to level of base knowledge.

■ Hooks in pre-work and provides greater challenge to outputs required for two-day workshop.

Is not:

■ Diageo-wide application (although now been adopted in the UK market).

■ Covering post-programme use (we are now looking at how to use/ adapt/embed learning after the workshop element and broaden the overall programme).

■ A simplistic tutorial.

■ A gimmick.

■ Optional pre-programme.

When we ran the e-impacted workshops, the design of the workshops did change – more exercises were used and we spent time with facilitators exploring the difference in their roles from an attitude/skills/knowledge perspective. Facilitators' views were that we could scale back the programme to one or one and a half days if we wanted to go down this route later.

What were the biggest challenges in setting them up and how did you overcome them?

Facilitators' acceptance of the change to workshop

I had to spend time setting up a commitment and then engaging them in the design and the specific areas they needed to focus on to change and to act as champions of the e-learning component. People had invested a lot of time in getting comfortable with rolling-out a workshop that was successful – this potentially was a risk.

How overcome? The special workshop on bringing blended learning into reality and onward engagement was time well spent to overcome possible resistance from within primarily the HR community.

Technology/IS support

We did not have a dedicated Global Supply IS support to the programme. We had a Diageo person checking the specs with the external provider but it still ran into problems. We had tracking mechanisms that forwarded to a nominated tutor so that we knew pre-work was being done. In some sites this did not work because of legacy systems.

How overcome? After the pilot we got our IS directors to test out some of the key mechanisms at various sites to ensure that they worked effectively. We also had some issues in the hand-over from our external supplier to our internal systems. We overcame this by going back to our supplier for more clarification about the technical infrastructure. It was a valuable lesson in recognizing the depth of knowledge required by the internal IS team in order for us to operate and maintain the system after an external supplier has completed their implementation.

Compulsory pre-work and consequences

We said that people must submit pre-work to attend the workshop. In the main people did this but it was last minute and they often needed the support of a local training person to answer questions.

How overcome? Buy-in from team leaders to endorse the importance of completing the pre-work and the consequences if they did not, and the role of the development person involved.

Time and ownership it takes for material redesign for the CD-ROM

We learnt from another project that we needed to own the material and the importance of using our own internal knowledge rather than relying on an external provider. To do this effectively we needed to allocate enough time to undertake the writing. We also needed to become guardians of our own intellectual property. As a result our development professionals needed to use a different set of capabilities.

How overcome? By allocating a set number of days, set people to write the content with the external provider's support.

What have been the benefits?

- Improvement in the application of high performance coaching.

- People are able to reference the Intranet site or CD-ROM several times for extra support.

- Standardization of knowledge base on a global scale for us.

- Material to work on with the embedding of the coaching capability onwards – especially dissemination to a wider audience.

What advice would you give to others?

- Be clear that you own the material and design even if you have a specialist company scripting for you. Plan out your own 'storyboard' style process before you go in to the proper process.

- Get an IS champion to support.

- Know what is in scope and out of scope for the project.

- Don't be seduced by the style of technology, ie video/audio – focus on the message and the language style appropriate to the culture/nature of your audience.

- Do a return on investment case.

- Make sure those impacted by running the new workshop are fully involved and engaged.

Any other comments?

We did this pilot with HPC and rolled out and are now doing the business case for e-learning within Supply. Therefore, the ROI was less focused than in to the future.

I had run a few potential user groups to assess their views, concerns, help in ideas on communication. There were not so many difficulties as first feared with people not being ready to learn in this way – probably because we were not 'short-changing' the face-to-face time in their eyes. However, this is a possible barrier we might have depending on the other programmes we work on and whether the social time gets eroded. This will be a company culture issue for many.

We had a quiz that needed to be answered and to a certain level. Some of the questions were very challenging and with some ambiguity in the answers. It was amazing the tenacity of people to get 100 per cent on the quiz. In the first version, it did not direct them back to the specific wrongly answered questions, causing considerable frustration. What a competitive lot we have!

For further information contact: claire.semple@diageo.com.

DAIMLERCHRYSLER UK LTD

DaimlerChrysler UK Ltd came into being in January 2000, reflecting the merger in 1998 of the German-based Daimler-Benz AG with the Chrysler Corporation in the US to form DaimlerChrysler AG. DaimlerChrysler UK has responsibility for the following brands in the UK: Mercedes-Benz – Passenger Cars and Commercial Vehicles, Maybach, Smart, Chrysler, Jeep and Mitsubishi Center.

The company is based in Milton Keynes and has responsibility for the sales, marketing, distribution and promotion of DaimlerChrysler products in the UK under the brand names listed above as well as for providing a host of support services to both our dealers and customers.

What examples do you have of blended learning?

Two examples. First, DaimlerChrysler has an extensive library of Computer Based Training (CBT) on technical subjects (car, van and truck systems and components) on CD-ROM. The target audience is technicians in dealership workshops. The initial modules of the CBTs also provide a technical understanding of systems for sales people.

Some of these offline CBTs are required pre-course work for attendance on face-to-face technical training. In the training course, trainers deliver theory and hands-on training on vehicles. The pre-course CBT covers basic theory needed to get the most out of the course (Example A).

Secondly, in 2000 we ran a pilot of a full online training course. It consisted of a time-tabled course run in Lotus Learning Space 4. It had an e-tutor and two classes of 10 delegates scattered around the UK. It used asynchronous communication via email and notice boards, and synchronous communication via the LLS virtual classroom and simultaneous telephone conference. Delegates who completed the online element qualified for the hands-on workshop. Very little theory was taught in the workshop as it had been covered in the online element. We have not been able to roll this out for reasons covered in the answers below (Example B).

What were the biggest challenges in setting it up?

(Example A)

1. The administration necessary to ensure that delegates have passed the relevant electronic assessment before gaining access to the face-to-face training.

2. Providing digestible instructions to busy people who are bombarded daily with directives and paperwork from head office.

3. The cultural shift for the training delegates' managers from sending people away for training to taking some responsibility to train on-site.

(Example B)

The above plus:

4. Technical support.

5. Firewalls (Internet deployment but accessed by users via our Extranet).

How did you overcome these?

Following the numbering above:

1. Mammoth effort by multiple parties to devise an administrative system, write and distribute to managers to follow up and keep records. Management buy-in essential.

2. A lot of re-writing of instructions and lots of telephone support.

3. We're still working on this one. Some businesses have taken quickly to the change, others will always resist it.

4. We decided the only way to overcome this factor was to employ a 'single box solution' with a central helpdesk. We cannot roll out full online learning to an audience with fragmented network, hardware and

software installations and support them. It was a full-time job just keeping 10 'clients' in contact.

5. Building relationships with those responsible in IT, learning about the technical issues and spending a lot of time fire fighting.

What have been the benefits?

(Example A)

- Completion of pre-course work ensures that all delegates come to the training with a guaranteed minimum level of knowledge.

- More training time can be spent working hands-on.

- More training time can be spent focusing on detail specific to the subject.

- The class is not kept waiting while the trainer helps a few delegates to catch up on basic knowledge.

- Delegates have the chance to cover the basic material at their own pace. Delegates have told us that this makes the training more interesting and useful for them but it only works if everyone has done the work.

(Example B)

- Spectrum of e-learning tools enhances existing methods of training.

- Carefully constructed blended solutions can offer a richer and more effective training package than traditional training alone.

- E-tutoring and peer group collaboration can be extremely powerful tools providing the best of both worlds.

- Building a learning culture and creating imperatives for learning remain the greatest challenge.

What advice would you give to others?

- Don't start with a solution which is looking for a problem. Analyse the training needs in your business and establish where a blended solution can add value for the trainee, the trainer and the business.

- Be practical and pragmatic.

- Think big and theoretical but act incrementally and in manageable, reversible steps.

AVIS EUROPE PLC

What examples do you have of blended learning?

We have been developing different approaches to induction over a number of years. One of our first developments was a multimedia package of about 13 hours. What we wanted to provide was a generic package, which could be delivered in a number of locations, but with the capacity to cater for local differences. We developed a multimedia programme for induction. The multimedia programme was supported by a learner guide, which is task-related, allowing local questions to be added. Our most recent work has been on using multimedia to assist in the induction of reservation agents in our call centre operations.

What were the biggest challenges in setting it up?

We are very decentralized. As the development evolved the business made a decision to bring the call centres, which had been located in nine different geographical locations, together in two locations, one in Barcelona covering Italy, France, Spain, Belgium, Portugal, Holland, and one in Manchester covering the UK, Austria, Germany and Switzerland. This meant that we had to cater for different languages, different cultures and also to recognize the practices that had been adopted locally. The content was quite diverse; everyone had been doing it slightly differently. This related to a very wide range of protocols, eg even in the first few sentences of answering a telephone. In some countries, cultural expectation drove the use of their name in the initial greeting. In others it is not and we had the ability to work their name into the conversation. The problem is how do you reflect this in one programme?

How did you overcome this?

What we recognized early on was that the multimedia approach could not be the only approach, it could never be able to be given all the local differences, but what it could do was contain the most common learning information that could then be supported by local variations, eg using our booking system and processing a voucher are standard, but what is available in a particular country may vary.

Another advantage was getting IT and Finance involved early on and helping us prepare a business case, which we developed based on cost savings rather than ROI as we felt in the early days it might be harder to prove to the executive the hard figures of ROI. We focused instead on identifying how the approach would save money. Initially our programmes for rental agents had achieved a large cost saving and paid for itself in less than one year.

What have been the benefits?

There have been many. Avis is developing an employment brand; this approach makes a major contribution to the development of the brand. We are able to build consistency in our approach. We have been able to integrate refresher training into the classroom; the tutor and student can dip into the information when they want it. We have also been able to build in flexibility with pure classroom training we would probably have kept people waiting until we had enough people to fill a course, now we can work with much smaller numbers. If someone misses a day they can easily catch up using the multimedia package. We have also been able to create more of a nursery environment, where people are supported while they learn to walk. The technology allows them to take calls and receive feedback, offering them guidance and encouragement, but then to also go back into the multimedia package to top up the information on key aspects of their development. It has allowed Training and Development to set themselves targets to achieve even more. It has opened people's eyes to the potential of doing things differently. There have been some hard benefits in terms of talk time and conversion; however, measuring the impact and attributing it directly to one source is difficult. Also, due to events (September 11) and economic factors, year on year improvements are difficult to achieve.

What advice would you give to others?

Talk to your IT department, involve them in what you are trying to do. Choose a partner (supplier) that you can work with and stay close to them. By close, I mean work with them, support them, challenge them, don't hand over a brief and expect the finished product to land in your lap as you would want it. It is possible to get over-excited and go way outside your brief, and the product will never get finished: focus on delivering the product. Technology is in continuous development; recognize that updating should be phased. Talk to your colleagues in the company about what you are doing. Use the people who have already completed the training in the more traditional format to test out the new approach that you are designing. Ask them to compare the new approach with the old – they will give fantastic feedback. Don't keep what you are developing to yourself: share it, encourage people to critique it. Taking feedback in the development stage is far more valuable when you can still amend it rather than later when valuable design time has been used. Involve the senior team – their support is critical.

Any other comments?

As a result of the success of this approach we are now looking at more pure online development to deliver other courseware, to look at our management and team development.

For further information contact: rob.field@avis-europe.com.

ASHRIDGE

Ashridge is a leading international business school. Our comprehensive portfolio of open executive education programmes – including innovative MBA, MSc and Diploma programmes – and our reputation as one of the world's leaders in tailored executive development are complemented by thriving organization consulting activities and application-orientated management research. Our international faculty, drawn from a rich diversity of backgrounds, combine their practical experience with academic knowledge. These strengths enable us to meet the development needs of both individual managers and leading organizations from around the world.

Many of our programmes, especially tailored ones, use a combination of classroom teaching, syndicate work, diagnostics, one-to-one coaching, feedback and e-learning. The e-learning includes access to content through the Virtual Learning Resource Centre (VLRC), online diagnostics and e-sharing facilities, which provide document stores and asynchronous bulletin board discussion. Many organizations with corporate universities are incorporating material from Ashridge's VLRC into their own blended learning programmes.

Tailored programmes

Recently we have delivered two programmes for clients where eLearning has been the central means of establishing the programme content. Pre-reading and interactive exercises were provided through a tailored Web application called 'eSharing'. The face-to-face element was then used to pick up on pre-work from the eLearning, give feedback and discuss more complex issues.

Another theme for tailored clients recently has been to use the eSharing application to facilitate virtual team activities and collaboration where documents are shared and work posted up for client sponsors to access.

Several tutors have commented that a more blended approach has given participants flexibility in terms of the amount of time participants allocate to exercises and preparation depending on their interest and requirements. It also frees up classroom time for more facilitative or one-to-one activites.

Open programmes

On the open course side we run a senior executive strategy and leadership programme four times a year. This programme was recently redesigned to make it slightly shorter, more modular and give it a more blended approach. It now incorporates pre-course preparation work using Web-based interactive learning objects. A typical learning object comprises 20 minutes of learning with up to six interactive exercises and illustrative multimedia examples. Participants are provided with a strategic tool-kit made up of eight learning objects, one for each strategic tool.

This is the self-paced element and ensures that all participants have the same understanding of the basic tools before the classroom sessions begin. Articles, PowerPoint presentations and handouts are available via a tailored Web application (eSharing). In between modules, course members can also share contact details including pictures and biographical details as well as participate in discussion on topical issues.

What have been the major challenges?

Culture and mindset

The biggest has been to change the existing mindset of Ashridge. Traditionally classroom teaching, syndicate work and one-to-one coaching have been the norm for Ashridge programmes, even though Ashridge has always been very innovative in its approach to learning. Several clients are now challenging this, especially on the tailored or customized side, requesting e-learning modules as part of the programme. Blended learning challenges traditional pricing models and reward structures.

How overcome? Internal marketing and raising awareness of the benefits has helped shift the culture as has increasing client demand. We have successfully adopted an incremental, almost drip-feed approach. More recognition is now being given for contributing content and supporting course members in online discussions. There have also been several development workshops around e-learning including the skills needed to successfully implement blended learning.

Team working

In order to deliver blended learning successfully, cross-functional teams need to come together. These teams need to include tutors, instructional designers, IT infrastructure specialists, Web/graphic designers, content managers and administrative support staff. This has been challenging for existing organizational structures.

How overcome? Job roles are flexible. Innovation is actively encouraged, and regular cross-disciplinary/functional team meetings and events are held. We have also appointed an e-learning consultant to assist with instructional design and to help coordinate the development of new blended learning initiatives across functions.

Engaging and supporting the learners

A further challenge relates to getting the learners on board and supporting them. This is a challenge especially with the online discussion forums. Also, as Ashridge tends to work with senior and middle managers IT literacy can be a barrier. In order for the e-learning element to be successful there has to be a close link between what is happening online and how it relates to the classroom sessions. The culture of the organization has a great impact on the ease with which this is adopted.

How overcome? Enormous energy has been put into helping customers market e-learning. This includes client visits and workshops, co-branding of brochures, mouse-mats, Post-its and posters. On the design front we have endeavoured to create seamless Web-based learning environments that are intuitive to the learner. We also provide online and telephone support.

Linked to the cultural issues, we are constantly reminding faculty that they need to work actively at supporting learners and finding creative ways of blending the technology with the classroom. Success stories are shared.

What have been the benefits?

For the clients and learners

■ The e-learning element of blended learning can save time and travel costs. We are in the process of redesigning our German consortium MBA to include two e-learning modules to reduce the time spent travelling between Germany and the UK.

■ Incorporating inter-modular e-learning in virtual teams reinforces this skill – geographically dispersed virtual teams are becoming more the norm in organizations of today.

■ The basic frameworks can be studied online before the course, freeing up time for more one-to-one sessions and practical activities in the classroom.

■ Learners can go at their own pace through some of the materials and select only those parts that they require.

■ The e-learning elements being accessible any time anywhere also increases the flexibility for learners over when and where they study.

For Ashridge

Delivering blended learning also encourages teamwork and multiskilling. We have several examples of Ashridge staff successfully redirecting their careers through multiskilling.

From a commercial perspective we are now better able to serve clients who request a blended approach to tailored programmes. We are also less constrained by the physical capacity at Ashridge nor as exposed to threats to the volume of business travel that events such as September 11 undoubtedly had.

What advice would you give to others?

- Manage customer expectations: it always takes longer than you think to develop e-learning materials.

- Be flexible in delivery channels: we have yet to find one ubiquitous Intranet. We offer access via the Internet, Intranet, CD or Lotus Notes technology.

- Marketing is crucial – need a drip-feed approach.

- In order to blend successfully you need to think how the e-learning elements feed into classroom sessions.

- Don't do with the technology what is clearly best done in the classroom.

- Keep the technology simple, using industry standards.

- It needs to be able to be personally tailored. We have many self-assessed diagnostic tools.

- Gimmicky technology is no substitute for good instructional design. Software should only be used if it adds to the learning experience.

- Deliver learning materials in short bite-sized chunks and be aware of how long managers will have to use it in reality.

- Think of e-learning as more than just content: support learners where possible as you would in the classroom.

- The e-learning element needs to be easily updateable and at least cosmetically tailorable.

For further information contact: andrew.ettinger@ashridge.org.uk or cath.redman@ashridge.org.uk.

BASIC SKILLS AGENCY

A new CD-ROM entitled 'Money-go-round', produced by the Basic Skills Agency and CNDL, has been developed to help people who have problems with reading and writing to understand the basics of everyday finance.

It is estimated that around 7 million adults in the UK have yet to acquire the literacy and numeracy skills that are expected of an average 11-year-old. Statistically, research has shown that this group is up to five times more likely to be unemployed and there are links between poor basic skills and financial exclusion and social disadvantage.

Aimed at an adult audience aged 25 years+, the content of the CD-ROM is underpinned by the new adult literacy/numeracy curriculum and concentrates on skills at entry level. The learning is focused on real world situations, offering a range of topics to equip people to organize their household finances, plan their spending, set up a bank account, deal with debt and much more.

Accompanied by a student and tutor guide booklet, the CD-ROM has been designed with the flexibility to be used in a supported group environment as well as by users working alone.

The challenges and solutions

One of the challenges faced in this blended learning project was to ensure that the learning was going to be truly flexible enough to be used by someone working in isolation, and as a tool for the tutor working with diverse groups.

To meet this challenge the content was broken into a number of RLOs (reusable learning objects), 'chunks' representing a single, intensive learning session. The great benefit of these RLOs is their flexibility. They can be assembled into a course string based on the results of a pre-learning quiz that identifies knowledge gaps in an individual user. Alternatively, a course string is set up by tutors to meet the needs of different learning groups, or RLOs can be selected at random.

Another challenge was to ensure that the learning remained accessible and appropriate for the target audience. It was critical to the success of the project that the users would not feel patronized in any way, and that the activities were relevant and useful to them.

To meet this challenge a focus group consisting of users, tutors, adult numeracy and literacy experts, and creative, technical and instructional designers was set up at the start of the project to ensure that the learning designed was going to meet these requirements. As a result of this iterative process, the design adopted had a friendly but serious style, with an interface that was simple, straightforward and 'non-technical'.

Lastly, it was critical that the adult numeracy and literacy tutors would be open to redesigning their coursework and using the learning activities on the CD-ROM. Again the focus group was instrumental by inviting tutors to evaluate the design and content from the early stages both as a group and through activities with existing literacy and numeracy schemes. As a result of this ownership, a key group of 'ambassadors' was created that was instrumental in making the tutors open to the idea of new practices.

The benefits

Users enjoy the flexibility of being able to work in isolation when embarrassed by their lack of skills, but can also enjoy being able to share and network with others in tutor-led sessions. The quiz proved particularly popular and clearly identifies individual learning needs. Users have also said that the activities make them feel that 'they are not the only one struggling'.

The focus group approach was a great success for the participants. Other networks were subsequently formed as a result of the original group to share ideas for future development of blended learning courses.

The iterative process, where feedback from the focus group was genuinely listened to and the creative and instructional design frequently amended, resulted in a product that was even more flexible than had been originally envisaged.

Lessons learnt

Having a focus group involved at all stages of the design will ensure that the learning meets the needs of the audience and that the product is successful. It can result, however, in some production issues, which might take longer to resolve than originally anticipated.

When using this approach we therefore recommended that time-scales should be stretched to allow for several reworks of both creative and instructional design. We also learnt that we should undertake a greater audit of what the tutors are doing currently in their classrooms before starting to design new digital activities to be blended in.

For further information contact: james@cndl-group.com.

COMPUTEACH INTERNATIONAL

Background

Computeach International delivers IT skills and industry-led qualifications assisting people to gain jobs in the computer industry. It is a leading distance learning company, using an inventory of paper-based learning products that are integrated with classroom-based courses. In 2002 it selected CNDL to convert its paper-based foundation courses to online delivery.

Computeach International looked to CNDL to efficiently integrate classroom events and online learning to allow it to reach a broader market and to add value to its successful paper-based distance learning books.

The challenges and solutions

One of the challenges faced in this integrated learning project was to ensure that online delivery added value to the excellent tried and tested existing paper-based courseware. We identified that there was a risk of compromising the value, given the complexity and detail of the subject matter.

To meet this challenge the production team worked closely with subject matter experts and the courseware authors to repurpose the book's 'chapters' into 100 RLOs (reusable learning objects), independent chunks of learning of about 15 minutes' duration. A range of appropriate interactions and exercises was then devised as a team and adopted by CNDL instructional designers to ensure that technology was used to its full advantage.

The online version, for example, was able to add value by allowing students to practise and use skills such as interacting with logic charts, rather than simply looking at examples in the book. The production process also included a large prototype/alpha phase in which Computeach authors and subject matter experts were able to trial and test a number of RLOs for accuracy, relevance and extended appeal before starting full-scale production.

Another challenge in this project was that CNDL was unable to access any of the target audience during production for evaluation purposes. As a result, we had to place an enormous amount of trust and faith in the client and their knowledge of the target audience. To meet this challenge we consulted fully with them at every stage of production.

The benefits

The end result will be a truly blended solution, with tutors monitoring student progress, supporting them with email and SMS text messages, creating individual course strings of digital learning courses for users and delivering classroom tuition and examinations.

Computeach foundation courses will become more flexible, easier to update, and should result in increased user pass rates and penetration into new markets. In addition to these familiar advantages, Computeach will benefit from a unique PR opportunity, of being able to offer to market the first truly integrated suite of computer skills courses.

Lessons learnt

This project taught us that to effectively repurpose existing distance learning material, it is critical to have the freedom to map the most appropriate delivery channel against the learning outcomes, and use the most effective interactive activities to deliver the learning. This focus on breaking the content into chunks and using the most appropriate medium for each chunk of learning means that you can produce a fully integrated approach that delivers more value and more user benefits than just the one method of delivery.

The success of this project also illustrated for us how integrating online learning with many different types of traditional and emerging teaching methods is the future.

For further information contact: james@cndl-group.com.

CDNL GROUP

CNDL is one of the UK's leading providers of high-value, bespoke e-learning content. At CNDL, we believe that an organization's major asset is its people and that tailored learning is the key to realizing the full potential of this resource. We have helped many leading companies to increase the efficiency of their workforce by providing them with award-winning, cost-effective e-learning solutions that work in the real world. Our reputation for providing engaging courseware is well known and we are currently developing solutions for some of the UK's most innovative learning projects.

NATIONWIDE TRUST

Nationwide Trust is the personal loans subsidiary of Nationwide Building Society, the UK's fourth largest mortgage lender and ninth largest retail banking, saving and lending organization. Nationwide Trust specializes in the provision of loan facilities to customers of Nationwide Building Society and also direct to the general public. Two products are provided; the Unsecured Personal Loan and the Secured Personal Loan. Each product is also available with optional protection cover.

Nationwide Trust is based in St Albans, Hertfordshire, with approximately 200 employees. There are also 15 Trust branches around the country, which act as processing and sales units as well as supporting Nationwide Building Society's 681 branches.

Nationwide Trust experienced a record year, to 4th April 2002, with gross advances of £692 million and outstanding loan balances increasing by £73 million to £1.2 billion. It has a current base of over 200,000 customers.

What examples do you have of blended learning?

We recently put together a customer service programme consisting of three parts:

1. CD online titles from Xebec McGraw-Hill, containing basic knowledge of the subject.

2. Classroom-type course for one day, putting the generic skills learnt from the CD online titles into specific use within our company.

3. More CD online titles from Xebec McGraw-Hill – more advanced customer service skills – dealing with angry customers, etc.

What were the biggest challenges in setting it up?

The main challenge was to ensure that all delegates had completed 1 (as above) before attending the course and ensuring they then completed 3 (as above) after the course, giving them a whole programme of customer service learning.

How did you overcome these?

Luckily, Xebec material has its own Management Information System and this automatically tracks the usage of titles against a user, so it was straightforward to see who had completed the titles and who had not.

What have been the benefits?

■ Cost-cutting – only a one-day course now rather than two days with an overnight stay.

E-learning culture – brought into the company as a result.

■ Blended learning – more opportunities to use this facility.

What advice would you give to others?

Ensure that when creating blended learning solutions, the training material doesn't overlap, otherwise it seems like you are forever covering the same areas and delegates may get bored. The blended learning effect is cost-effective, easy to understand and can bring businesses up to date with the technological advances out there.

Any other comments?

The final point is to remember that everyone has their own preferred learning style – this may not suit everyone, but it will allow you to have more scope and to use your creative skills to create the best training options that you can.

For further information contact: jomas@whitler.fsnet.co.uk.

THE US DEPARTMENT OF HEALTH AND HUMAN SERVICES

What examples do you have of blended learning?

We are currently developing a Department-wide supervisory training blended solution. Based on several currently offered classroom courses, we are surveying managers and supervisors on 'e-learning readiness' and re-validating their perceptions of what they need correlating that with the government-wide competencies identified by the US Office of Personnel Management (www.opm.gov).

We have then allocated about $100,000 to build out a demonstration module usable by the different programs. We have access to SkillSoft's interpersonal library and NETg courseware through our Distributed Learning Network (DL\net) (www.learning.hhs.gov) which uses THINQ as its LMS. We also have been using Achieve Global's Frontline Leadership and Leadership for Results modules. The latter product has e-learning versions which may be incorporated into the learning solution.

What were the biggest challenges in setting them up?

Mostly political for us, since we have build a robust infrastructure with over 300 courses, a 'communities of practice' function that includes a variety of collaborative tools to support learning (available on the DL\net), and the ability to customize and track curriculum completion through the LMS certification.

How did you overcome these?

As Mme. DeFarge noted in Dickins' *A Tale of Two Cities*: 'Still knitting.'

What have been the benefits?

As of this writing, it has forced different parts of the Department to focus on more coherent training solutions due to the need to train more efficiently and due to the cost of development of these kinds of learning modules.

What advice would you give to others?

Build your infrastructure first. After that, it becomes an ISD and evaluation issue. Otherwise, you will be fighting with your IT people. Also, address any compatibility and 508 (Federal handicapped access issues) very early in your process. They can kill the whole show.

Any other comments?

Bonne chance!

THINQ LIMITED

THINQ Limited is the leading provider of enterprise learning management systems (LMS) with more large-scale deployments than any other LMS vendor, including 23 customers with more than 23,000 learners and 12 customers with more than 70,000. THINQ delivers proven enterprise and extra-enterprise learning management solutions that improve employee and organizational readiness and achievement through effective human capital development. The THINQ TrainingServer LMS empowers corporations and government agencies to improve performance, adapt to change and advance their most important business goals. Customers including the PwC and HMCE use the THINQ LMS, combined with THINQ's broad content and professional services, to power their businesses' learning programmes on a global scale. THINQ is a private company with operations in the UK, the US and Canada.

For more information visit: www.THINQ.com.

WHAT LESSONS HAVE WE LEARNT FROM THE CASE STUDIES?

One of the key lessons is the range and variety of blended learning applications. Although many companies are only just beginning to be aware of the real potential of blended learning the examples in this chapter are actively embracing the opportunity and although there are very real challenges, there are also some very exciting opportunities being opened up by this approach.

The lessons are summarized here and also in Chapter 8. Some of the key points raised are as follows:

- Protect and recognize the importance of intellectual property.

- Value your own skills and knowledge internally.

- Use external support appropriately, keeping ownership.

- Follow the process through, asking deep and probing questions of your suppliers, making sure that they troubleshoot during the implementation process.

- Involve senior people in the sponsoring process.

- Remember everyone has a preferred learning style: aim to provide learning that allows every learner to experience his or her own style as part of the learning process, but also encourage experimentation outside of his or her comfort zone.

- Build in focus groups and take feedback from experienced learners.

- Be aware of what already exists: undertake an audit of the current provision.

- Manage customer expectations: it always takes longer than you think to develop e-learning materials. In order to blend successfully you need to think how the e-learning elements feed into classroom sessions.

- Choose a partner (supplier) that you can work with and stay close to them. By close, I mean work with them, support them, challenge them – don't hand over a brief and expect the finished product to land in your lap as you would want it.

■ Don't do with the technology what is clearly best done in the classroom.

■ Keep the technology simple, using industry standards.

Finally, I would like to thank all the individuals and organizations mentioned above for their willingness to be involved with these case studies, and for sharing both the highlights and the challenges.

7

Building learning networks

One of the real challenges in introducing blended learning is that the potential is so far reaching and awesome that it is possible to get carried away with the excitement of what can be achieved. As with any major initiative it is really important to recognize the reality of the start point and to plan the implementation carefully. The process highlighted in Chapter 2 is the first step and Chapter 3 takes it further, but the real impact in a personal sense will be felt by those who are responsible for sponsoring and steering the organization through the process.

Managing a large-scale implementation process will be an exciting but potentially frustrating and challenging task. The interpersonal relationships involved, the influencing, making the connections between the different types of learning and building positive relationships with providers will mean that whoever is involved needs to manage their own work pattern to achieve a sense of balance.

SELF-KNOWLEDGE

- How well do you know yourself?

- Can you accurately describe your strengths and areas of development?

- Do you really understand how you will react in different circumstances?

- Do you listen to advice from other people?

■ Have you received feedback that has helped you to gain insight into your personality or the way you react to others?

■ Are you someone that others turn to? Do you inspire trust; do you help others through the tough times? Giving an impression of quiet confidence can inspire others. What could you do to be more consistent in your support?

■ How aware are you of your communication style? Would others describe you as an effective communicator?

■ How easy do you find it to switch off? How often do you take time to socialize with others informally both in and out of work?

■ Do you seek to broaden your perspective by taking time to mix with people with different interests, backgrounds, people who may challenge you?

The more insight you gain the better able you are to self-motivate and to harness your energy and talents to achieve your dreams. Many hopes and dreams never come to fruition because people make it too difficult for themselves to achieve them. The greater your self-knowledge the more able you are to create the situations and to identify the support that will help you to help others.

Creative, artistic and busy professional people are potentially susceptible to 'burn out'. Prevention is better than cure and all the measures mentioned below are relevant. Equally, with experience you are better able to manage your work/life pressures to achieve a balance. There are specific actions that you can take to minimize the risk; this list may also be relevant to your learner:

■ Get to know yourself: find out how much sleep you need on a regular basis and try to achieve at least an average number of hours' sleep per week.

■ Eat properly: find a diet that gives you the proper balance of foods for your lifestyle.

■ Take some form of exercise: choose something that you can do regularly and which gives you an opportunity to meet other people.

- Develop a network of professional colleagues and friends who you can use to support you. Particularly important are people who motivate and inspire you, or who make you laugh; humour is a great stress reliever.

- Regularly undertake professional development: identify new skills or areas of expertise.

- Each day create space, however little, just for yourself. Whatever other work or domestic pressures exist take time to devote to yourself. Use it to do something relaxing, read a book, listen to music, telephone someone, clear something from your personal action list, or just stare into space.

- Recognize your achievement: it's wonderful when other people give you positive feedback, but reviewing your own progress can equally be positive, particularly if you have logged your starting point.

- Be alert to the signals of too much pressure and do something before you reach the symptoms of stress.

- Build variety into your working life: try not to fall into the routine of, 'I'm coaching Jane therefore it must be Thursday.'

- Set yourself lifetime goals and regularly review progress against them.

TAKE TIME TO TALK

Who do you talk to? By this I do not mean gossip, or idle chit chat, but really talk to in a way that actually means something. The sale of mobile phones increases every day, all the telecommunications companies are competing for your air time and yet if you analysed the time you spend on the phone and the size of your phone bill and asked yourself if it really made you or the person on the other end of the line feel better you may find a surprising result. This is particularly true of mobile phones: you are more likely to come off the phone completely frustrated and exhausted at being cut off every time you lose a signal.

Contrast that with the feeling you get when you sit down and talk with someone you care for, or someone who has really listened to you, given you valuable advice, or simply made you laugh. We are told that the art of conversation is dead: in the age of the email we converse in broken sentences, blunt and to the point, and yet even email can be used to link families across the globe to allow children to communicate with parents, to allow business people to talk to their families.

Talking to people by whatever means is vitally important: it is a lifeline that can stimulate your mind, bring happiness and security knowing that you have people who care. When people experience dramatic changes in their work or lifestyle they are often encouraged to talk to people in their network; it is then that you may find that you have far fewer people to talk to than you realized. It is better to start growing your network now than wait until a crisis triggers it. When you email people in your business network remember they are human, and try to remember information about them that is important to them. Ask them how their projects are going; if you find something inspiring email the link to them, not annoying chain emails but something unique and special.

MANAGE YOUR OWN SUCCESS

If you believe in yourself it is much easier to convince others to believe in you. Self-belief comes from within; others can reinforce it, but first you need to plant the seed. Every national sports team develops confidence by encouraging team members to understand their individual strengths. The team coach works to build personal strength, team cohesion and belief in their ability to win. If you are really going to help others achieve their personal learning goals you need to believe in your own ability, you need to develop an inner resilience to help you keep going through difficult times.

There is a strong belief by the writers of many personal development and self-help books that if you really believe in something you can make it happen: it is the power of positive thought. If you believe in the power of positive thought you are more likely to be able to support others develop their own self-belief.

If you are going to be involved with a major implementation of blended learning, it would be very easy to lose sight of your own personal objectives, so it is important for you to identify how it might fit with your own goals. As a starting point you may like to review the following questions:

- What is my personal vision?

- What would I like to do next?

- What are my SMART objectives?

- Who do I know who can help me?

- What are the key actions that will help me?

- What might stop me?

- How can I reinforce the activities that will help me?

- How can I overcome what might stop me?

- What is the first thing that I am going to do to get started?

- How will I know that I have been successful?

After you have achieved your own personal goal:

- Recognize your achievement.

- Review it against your objectives and action plan.

- Make sure you capture all your memories and successes and what you have learnt about how you prefer to learn.

- Talk to your own coach and your network; let them know what you have achieved, thank them for their support.

- Plan what you want to do next.

- Start the same process of setting goals and outlining your next SMART objectives.

- Celebrate what you have achieved!

BUILD A SUPPORT NETWORK

In today's working environment there is less and less time for people to think, to talk to their colleagues and to reflect on what they are trying to do with their lives. Building a support network is one way of identifying people with whom you can develop an ongoing relationship, which enables you to explore your personal thoughts in more depth. You need someone who will help you to achieve insights, who will continue to be there for you over a period of time.

What distinguishes this approach from coaching, counselling or mentoring is the informality of it: the boundaries are agreed between the individuals and it may happen completely outside any form of structured training and organization development. In many ways these people are guides, or fellow travellers on the way to similar destinations. Talk to anyone who has travelled around the world and they will recount times and places where they met other travellers who shared wisdom about potential pitfalls or equally valuable information about where to stay or places to visit.

If you are not naturally comfortable with the concept of networking, start in a way that feels right for you. Networking is not just a one-way process: people will equally want you in their network. It is all part of the philosophy of helping others. Effective networking requires a lightness of touch, which is based on helping each other and sharing good fortune.

People who are skilled at networking have a network of people who range from those who are very close to those with whom they have less contact but who they can call upon for help if required. The best networks are the ones that are reciprocal and where it is fun to be a member.

Networking with people who are implementing blended learning can be equally valuable. Everyone is on a journey of discovery; the willingness of people to share information is very evident in the case studies in Chapter 6. The advances in technology, the speed with which new capabilities are being discovered, all add dimensions to the learning experience.

Talking to others involved in implementation can yield really valuable information. Everyone has the opportunity to hold conversations with a number of people, selected on the basis of a desire to learn from each other and a shared interest, and increasingly a desire to spend time with each other. Time for conversations initially may be at a premium and so the very nature of choosing who you want to spend time with becomes increasingly important. Equally, because there is freedom of choice, meetings are set up by mutual agreement. In some cases this may happen outside the working environment. If people perceive it to be of value, then they will make time for it. What can also happen is that people can have a number of people who they meet with, sharing different conversations and so widening and enriching the experience. In the context of blended learning the implementations are happening in a global context, so you may just as likely be emailing to a colleague in another time zone, with very different, or very similar, implementation challenges, or you may benefit from the knowledge that they have already gathered.

One very important aspect of this type of networking is commitment to follow up when required. It is very easy to meet, have a great conversation full of richness, both agree to do things and then to meet again, possibly several months later and nothing has happened. On the surface that is absolutely fine, and that might be appropriate in some types of situations. However, agreeing ground rules about follow up, or committing to find out further information before the next meeting, or sending information to each other can enrich the overall experience.

SHARE INFORMATION

You may also want to consider sharing your own experiences in implementing blended learning. As illustrated by the case studies, there are many ways in which you can share information with others about the work that you are doing. Often people forget to share their successes or to learn from each other's experiences. Build in opportunities to share information, both internally and externally. Run seminars, workshops, or input into other people's learning events.

USEFUL CONTACTS

There are many providers of e-learning information, but one organization that provides an international source of useful information about e-learning is the MASIE Center, which hosts the TechLearn and The World e-Learning Congress: www.masie.com.

Another organization is WOLCE. The WOLCE event celebrated its 10th birthday on 2/3 October 2002 at the NEC Birmingham by taking on a new name. The event is now called The World of Learning Conference and Exhibition, the 'open learning' part of the title having been replaced with 'of Learning'. Its research indicated that 89 per cent of all senior training professionals advocate using blended solutions to complete the rounded training package they offer to their companies. The WOLCE event will now encompass all delivery methods of training, which will not only be reflected by the exhibiting companies but also in the conference programme. For more information contact: www.wolce.com.

Also get in touch with your regional professional associations, many of which will have useful contacts on e- and blended learning.

8

So where do we go from here?

Traditionalists should remember the only way to fail is not to try and try we must. (Ridderstrale and Nordstrom, *Funky Business*)

The reality is that no one knows what new development is around the corner. Learning is all about evolving, growing and gaining wisdom. For learning professionals the excitement and challenges arise when new opportunities are presented to create learning experiences that are special for our learners.

The potential of blended learning is enormous and could represent the most fundamental overhaul of learning ever undertaken by your organization, but like any major initiative it needs significant investment, dedicated personnel and sponsorship at the highest level. Carefully handled, the potential cost savings and ROI could build a very compelling argument that any executive would find hard to resist.

In the enthusiasm to embrace the potential of online learning or other multimedia options it is important to recognize the wider opportunities to review and update the whole learning experience. As highlighted in earlier chapters, an important part of the development of blended learning is asking the following questions and applying them to all learning and development:

■ Given the breadth and depth of the learning experience that we can offer, which method or process will provide the most appropriate and stimulating learning experiences for our learners?

- Recognizing the different learning styles and multiple intelligences highlighted in Chapter 2, are there different ways in which we can present the same information so that we can provide the greatest choice for our learners?

- Can we challenge some deeply held perceptions of how learning can be delivered to broaden its scope and engage our learners in a different way?

- Can we also support our learning and development colleagues and encourage them to experiment with different ways of transferring the learning?

- Can we share the information positively with our line managers so that they respond and support their team members in developing new ways of learning?

- Can we present a persuasive business case for our corporate sponsors so that the executive feel confident in endorsing the investment?

WHAT ARE THE BENEFITS OF BLENDED LEARNING?

Using online learning within a blended solution helps to focus on the individual and their interaction with learning technologies using the Internet or Intranet.

There are a number of advantages to be gained from using blended learning in its various forms:

- learning can be more targeted, focused, delivered bite-size, just-in-time;

- learners can interact with the tutor;

- learners can interact with their peers;

- learning materials are readily accessible;

- a variety of techniques can be utilized by maximizing different technologies;

- it can build on other off-the-job provision.

There are very few disadvantages, but there are aspects to be aware of when introducing blended learning:

- launch it online and offline;

- identify the support networks, both technical helplines and coaching support;

- encourage learners to announce when they are engaged in online learning so that they are not interrupted;

- encourage learners to recognize how they learn best, and that they should create a learning environment that works for them, at work or at home;

- encourage learners to share successes and support each other;

- create learning that is stimulating, visually compelling and recognizes different learning styles;

- integrate online learning with other forms of learning.

WHAT IS THE FUTURE FOR BLENDED LEARNING?

The future for blended learning will very much depend on the pace of change in your organization and the level of commitment to doing things differently. Introducing the online components of blended learning does require investment, but the cost savings could be significant in the longer term. It also represents a very positive way of targeting learning and development, but it requires sponsorship and commitment at the highest level to really exploit its full potential.

On the technology front there are new developments all the time: some will work and others may be more experimental. One of the opportunities for online learning in the future is the development of hand-held devices or PDAs (Personal Digital Assistants). Using wireless technology the PDA has the potential to provide mobile access to e-learning content. The growth of the use of mobiles providing a range of functions means that in time learning could be available via an individual's mobile phone. Learning could be adapted from the PC to a hand-held machine; if this is the case the learning would need to be tailored even further. Already text messages are a very popular form of communication and a similar technology could be developed to share learning content. If organizations are committed to providing online learning there will be a need to explore different ways of accessing the material, particularly in areas such as manufacturing, retail and catering.

WHAT LESSONS HAVE WE LEARNT TO DATE?

I asked the people involved with the case studies for their comments, and here are some of the points they have made based on their experiences:

> Be clear that you own the material and design even if you have a specialist company scripting for you. Plan out your own 'storyboard' style process before you go in to the proper process. Get an IS champion to support.
> Know what is in scope and out of scope for the project.
> Don't be seduced by the style of technology, ie video, audio – focus on the message and the language style appropriate to the culture/nature of your audience. Do a return on investment case.
> Make sure those impacted by running the new workshop are fully involved and engaged.

> In looking at the self-study parts of a blended solution, the design is an important feature. In the classroom environment, a good presenter can make up for poor design of learning materials – in self-study mode it is much more important for the content to be engaging, well-structured and interactive (ie, forcing the user to think about what they are doing – not just clicking through a presentation or electronic book).

> The existing standards are focused on getting the technologies talking to each other – so it is important for making the linkages work that the learning content 'talks to' the learning management system, and that user records for achievement and progress can be exchanged between the learning package and the management system. However, none of the standards recognize whether the learning design is any good – the content might be SCORM-compliant but actually be completely ineffective as a learning tool.

The other thing that I would highlight – but it may be more of an issue for larger organizations with dedicated training resource – is that it is important to build up a common understanding of what e-learning is, and how it can be utilized in training/learning programme design. Otherwise you get an inconsistent message about what is trying to be achieved, and actual damage being done inadvertently by one part of the organization to another, eg, 'Oh I wouldn't recommend e-learning because it is expensive' or, 'E-learning doesn't work – it's not as good as traditional methods' – both of which are paraphrases of comments which could easily be argued the other way around depending on the circumstances or specific example used.

Include a timeline in the action plan and do not underestimate the time it takes to implement certain solutions. Best to find out from the technology vendor the time needed to implement a particular solution. Many times large implementations have a phased approach so as to get immediate training needs up and running and then bring on more technology and learners as the implementation progresses. Scale of project is also important to consider.

Talk to other people in the company, share what you are doing, invite feedback, involve the senior team, their support is critical.

Remember that everyone has their own preferred learning style – this may not suit everyone, but it will allow you to have more scope and to use your creative skills to create the best training options that you can.

Ensuring that a focus group is involved at all stages of the design will ensure that the learning meets the needs of the audience, and that the product is successful. It can result, however, in some production issues, which might take longer to resolve than originally anticipated.

When using this approach we therefore recommended that time-scales should be stretched to allow for several reworks of both creative and instructional design. We also learnt that we should undertake a greater audit of what the tutors are doing currently in their classrooms before starting to design new digital activities to be blended in.

Manage customer expectations; it always takes longer than you think to develop e-learning materials.

Be flexible in delivery channels; we have yet to find one ubiquitous Intranet. We offer access via the Internet, Intranet, CD or Lotus Notes technology.

Marketing is crucial – you need a drip-feed approach. In order to blend successfully you need to think how the e-learning elements feed into classroom sessions. Don't do with the technology what is clearly best done in the classroom. Keep the technology simple, using industry standards.

It needs to be able to be personally tailored. We have many self-assessed diagnostic tools. Gimmicky technology is no substitute for good instructional design. Software should only be used if it adds to the learning experience.

Deliver learning materials in short bite-sized chunks and be aware of how long managers will have to use it in reality. Think of e-learning as more than just content, support learners where possible as you would in the classroom. The e-learning element needs to be easily updateable and at least cosmetically tailorable.

Ensure that when creating blended learning solutions, the training material doesn't overlap otherwise it seems like you are forever covering the same areas and delegates may get bored. The blended learning effect is cost-effective, easy to understand and can bring businesses up to date with the technological advances out there.

Talk to your colleagues in the company about what you are doing. Use the people who have already completed the training in the more traditional format to test out the new approach that you are designing, ask them to compare the new approach with the old, they will give fantastic feedback. Don't keep what you are developing to yourself, share it, encourage people to critique it; taking feedback in the development stage is far more valuable when you can still amend it than later when valuable design time has been used. Involve the senior team – their support is critical.

Don't start with a solution that is looking for a problem. Analyse the training needs in your business and establish where a blended solution can add value for the trainee, the trainer and the business. Be practical and pragmatic.

Think big and theoretical but act incrementally and in manageable, reversible steps.

Above all remember the need to remain focused on the *learner*. Perhaps the biggest danger in any 'e' or blended solution project is becoming focused on technology/creativity, and not the audience. It is important that the learners' needs are fully captured and documented at the start of the project and that any success measures are based around these.

ARE YOU READY FOR BLENDED LEARNING?

If you are considering a blended learning approach you may want to ask yourself the following questions:

- Do you want to give your employees:
  - the opportunity to undertake an online assessment that identifies the way they prefer to learn?
  - the time to take that information and talk through the implications with their line manager who has time to spend on their development?
  - the opportunity to only have to attend the training that they select from generic programmes to build their own personal skill base?
  - a route to select personal development actions that meet their exact learning needs?
  - a means of tracking their own learning and building a personal portfolio?
  - the opportunity to undertake their own development at a time, place and pace to suit them?
- Do you want to give line managers:
  - all of the above but in addition. . .
  - the opportunity to select targeted, focused learning for their team members?

- time to coach and develop on a one-to-one basis?

- a flexible approach to their own learning?

■ Is your organization ready for:

- a dynamic partnership between your employees and the organization, where individual skills and behaviours are aligned to corporate goals and objectives, supported by a relationship with quality suppliers providing the very latest competitively priced online learning and development?

- the opportunity to create a positive employer brand offering all employees the opportunity to align their own development to the overall direction of the business and to be supported as they work towards achieving their own goals, hopes and aspirations?

■ Do you want to be:

- inspired, excited, stimulated and motivated about not just the learning opportunities that you will create for others, but also the learning that you will undertake for yourself?

- able to network on a virtual and global basis, linking internationally with other forward-looking learning and development professionals?

- able to create your own best practice environment where you can build your own case studies based on the successes that you have achieved and the lessons you have learnt?

- someone who makes a difference and is part of a world class learning revolution that will change the way learning and development is delivered forever?

If you have answered yes to a high proportion of the questions above then blended learning may present you with an opportunity to experiment with a new way of addressing the needs of your learners, and give you some very interesting opportunities to grow your own skill set.

The people who achieve something truly unprecedented have more than enormous talent and intelligence. They have original minds. They see things differently. They want to do the next thing, not the last one. (Bennis and Biedermann, *Organizing Genius*)

I hope this book and the case studies have inspired you to explore the potential of blended learning, and I wish you every success in your journey of discovery.

Recommended reading

Belasco, J A (1990) *Teaching the Elephant to Dance: Empowering change in your organisation*, Hutchinson Business, London

Belbin, M B (1981) *Management Teams*, Heinemann, Oxford

Bennis, W and Biedermann, P W (1997) *Organizing Genius*, Nicholas Brealey, London

Bissell, P and Barker, G (1988) *A Better Mousetrap: A guide for inventors*, Wordbase Publications, West Yorkshire

Black, J (1994) *Mindstore*, Thorsons, London

Bohm, D and Nicol, L (1996) *On Dialogue*, Routledge, London

Buzan, T (1995) *Use Your Head*, 4th edn, BBC, London

Buzan, T and Buzan, B (1993) *The Mind Map Book*, BBC, London

CBI in association with KPMG (2001) *Intellectual Property: A business guide*, CBI, London

Csikzentmihalyi, M (1990) *Flow*, Harper & Row, London

de Bono, E (1999) *Six Thinking Hats*, Little Brown, Boston, MA

Dyson, J (1998) *Against the Odds: An autobiography*, Trafalgar Square, London

Gardner, H (1993) *Frames of Mind*, Basic Books, New York

Goleman, D (1999) *Working with Emotional Intelligence*, Bloomsbury, London

Handy, C (1994) *The Empty Raincoat*, Hutchinson, London

Handy, C (1995) *Beyond Certainty*, Hutchinson, London

Heller, R (1998) *In Search of European Excellence*, HarperCollins Business, London

Helmstetter, S (1998) *What to Say When You Talk to Yourself*, Cynus, London

Jaworski, J and Senge, P (1998) *Synchronicity*, Berrett-Koeler, London

Kanter, R M (1983) *The Change Masters*, Allen and Unwin, London

Kanter, R M (1989) *When Giants Learn to Dance*, Simon and Schuster, London

Kao, J (1996) *Jamming: The art and discipline of business creativity*, HarperCollins, London

Kolb, D A, Rubin, I M and McIntyre, J M (1994) *Organizational Psychology: An experiential approach to organisational behavior*, 4th edn, Prentice Hall, London

LeBoeuf, M (1976) *Creative Thinking*, Piatkus, London

McNally, D (1993) *Even Eagles Need a Push*, Thorsons, London

O'Connor, J and Seymour, J (1990) *Introducing NLP: Neuro linguistic programming*, Mandala, London

O'Connor, J and Seymour, J (1994) *Training with NLP: Skills for managers, trainers and communicators*, Thorsons, London

Peters, T (1992) *Liberation Management*, Macmillan, Basingstoke

Peters, T (1997) *The Circle of Innovation*, Hodder & Stoughton, London

Peters, T and Austin, N (1985) *A Passion for Excellence*, Collins, London

Rawlinson, G 'How to invent almost anything – an easy introduction to the art and science of innovation', available at Graham@dagr.demon.co.uk

Redfield, J (1998) *The Celestine Vision*, Bantam Books, London

Redfield, J and Adrienne, C (1995) *The Celestine Prophecy – An experiential guide*, Bantam Books, London

Ridderstrale, J and Nordstrom, K (2000) *Funky Business*, ft.com

Salovey, P, Mayer, J D and Caruso, D R (1997) 'Emotional Intelligence Meets Traditional Standards for an Intelligence', unpublished manuscript

Semler, R (1993) *Maverick*, Arrow, London

Senge, P M (1990) *The Fifth Discipline*, Doubleday, New York

Slater, R (1998) *Jack Welch and the GE Way – Management insights and leadership secrets of the legendary CEO*, McGraw-Hill, Maidenhead

Thorne, K (2001) *Personal Coaching: Releasing potential at work*, Kogan Page, London

Thorne, K (2001) *Managing the Mavericks*, Chandos, London

Thorne, K and Machray, A (2000) *World Class Training – Providing training excellence*, Kogan Page, London

Thorne, K and Mackey, D (2001) *Everything You Ever Needed to Know About Training*, 2nd edn, Kogan Page, London

Torrance, P (1995) *Why Fly? A philosophy of creativity*, Ablex Publishing, Westport, Conn

Also published by Kogan Page

Collis, B and Moonen, J (2001) *Flexible Learning in a Digital World*

Inglis, A, Ling, P and Joosten, V (2002) *Delivering Digitally*, 2nd edn

Jolliffe, A, Ritter, J and Stevens, D (2001) *The Online Learning Book*

Salmon, G (2000) *E-moderating: The key to teaching and learning online*

Index

activists 22, 23
Advanced Distributed Learning
    (ADL) 13
Application Service Provider (ASP)
    13
appraisals 75
Ashridge 104–08
asynchronous communication
    97
audio–conferencing 11
Avis 101–03

Basic Skills Agency 109–11
benchmarking 67
blended learning
    approach to 41–43
    benefits 132–33
    business strategy 28–34, 77
    definition 16–17
    demand for 37
    designing 55–73, 83, 134
    drawbacks 17–18
    lessons from 134–37
    management support for 30–31
    meaning 1–2, 10–17
    obstacles 84–86
    selecting a provider 34
    timeliness 137–38

brain 24–28
    left 25
    right 25
brainstorming 63
'brand concept' 9
'branding' 7–10 see also employer
    brand
'burn out' 124
business case 30, 77, 96, 102, 132
Buzan, Tony 25, 63

case studies 87–121
    Ashridge 104–08
    Avis 101–03
    Basic Skills Agency 109–11
    Computeach 112–14
    Daimler–Chrysler 97–100
    Diageo 92–96
    lessons from 120–21
    Nationwide Trust 115–16
    Rolls Royce 88–91
    THINQ Limited 119
coaching see personal coaching
communication 9, 47, 124, 125–26
    asynchronous 97
    synchronous 97
company culture 36, 77, 105–06
Computeach 112–14

confidentiality agreements   67
creativity   56–63
   stages of   60–63
   tools and techniques   63–65
cross-functional working   7, 32, 106
Csikzentmihalyi, Mihalyi   57
customers   7–8, 9, 61

Daimler Chrysler   97–100
De Bono, Edward   63
Diageo   92–96
Disney   64, 71
'displayed thinking'   64, 71

e-commerce   69
e-learning   1, 10–11, 12, 29, 37–38,
   130
e-mail   18
emotional intelligence   6, 26–28
employer brand   7–10, 102
evaluation   40, 43, 79, 82– 83, 90

failure, fear of   56–57
focus groups   110–11, 120, 135
feedback   75–76, 124
'flow'   57–58
flowcharts   65
Foote, Nathaniel   15

Gardner, Howard   20, 25, 27
   seven intelligences   25–26
Goleman, Daniel   20, 26–28, 62, 63
   emotional competencies   27
   see also emotional intelligence

Handy, Charles   20

IMS   14, 71
information sharing   129, 132

inspiration, sources of   58–60
Internet   12, 65, 72
Intranet   12
intuition   6
intellectual property   15, 66–67, 95,
   120
IT infrastructure   29

jargon   10
'just-in-time' learning   16, 132

Kolb, David   19, 20, 21, 24, 37
knowledge management   14–16, 65

leadership   6
learning contract   69–70
learning cycle   21–22, 48
learning environment   19, 49–52,
   61, 85
Learning Management System
   (LMS)   12–13, 34, 84, 119, 134
learning networks   123–30
learning objectives   12, 36, 38–39,
   42 see also personal objectives
learning organization   50
learning portals   12
learning, pre-school/early years   29
learning, reflecting on   76–80
learning resources centres   40
learning styles   19–20, 22, 24, 28,
   37, 43, 76, 83, 120, 132, 135
lifelong learning   21
line manager, role of   48–49

Manville, Brook   15
MASIE Center   130
Mayer, John   27
mind mapping   72
Mind Maps® technique   25, 63

monitoring arrangements 43 *see also* evaluation
multimedia technology 16, 70–71, 101

Nationwide Trust 115–16
networking 128–29

online learning
  communities 12
  designing 66–69
  infrastructure 49
  providers 33–34
online text animation 16
organizational culture *see* company culture

partnership working 8
performance measurement 8
personal coaching 20, 36, 39, 43, 44, 50–51
  environment 49–53
personal development 123–27
  model of 43–46
Personal Digital Assistant (PDA) 14, 133–34
personal objectives 127
personal profiling 45, 46
Podolny, Joel 85
Poincaré, Jules Henri 62
pragmatists 22, 23
problem-solving 64–65 *see also* creativity
psychometric tests 45, 46
'push/pull' theory 15

recruitment and retention 6, 62
reflection 52–53
  on learning 76–80

reflectors 22, 23
Rolls Royce 88–91

Salovey, Peter 27
SCORM (Shareable Content Object Reference Model) 13–14, 71
self-belief 126
self-knowledge 123–25
Semler, Sicardo 6
Six Thinking Hats 63
standards 8
storyboards 65, 95
support network 128–29
SWOT analysis 52
synchronicity 6
synchronous communication 11–12, 97

team working 64–65, 106 *see also* cross-functional working
theorists 22, 23
Theta process 58
THINQ Limited 119
Torrance, Paul 20, 60
trainer, role of 47–48, 50
training needs analysis (TNA) 32–33, 39, 41, 77, 78, 79, 80–84
  cost-effectiveness 81–84
  elements of 80–81

US Department of Defense (DoD) 13
US Department of Health and Human Services 117–18

values 8
video-conferencing 11
virtual classroom 11, 16, 71–73, 104

virtual teams   72, 107
vision   8
visualization   63–64
voicemail   16

WAP (Wireless Application
   Protocol)   14

WBT (Web-based Training)   11
Web designers   38, 65, 66
Web sites   11
wheel of life   44, 46
WOLCE (World of Learning
   Conference and Exhibition)
   130